Christian Perspectives
on
Development Issues

Series Editor: Enda McDonagh

REFUGEES
AND FORCIBLY
DISPLACED PEOPLE

Mark Raper SJ
and Amaya Valcárcel

TRÓCAIRE   VERITAS   CAFOD   SCIAF

TRÓCAIRE

Catholic Agency for World Development,
169 Booterstown Avenue,
Blackrock, Co. Dublin, Ireland.

Tel: +353 1 288 5385
Fax: +353 1 288 3577
e-mail: info@trocaire.ie
http://www.trocaire.org

VERITAS

Veritas House,
7-8 Lr Abbey Street,
Dublin 1, Ireland.

Tel: +353 1 878 8177
Fax: +353 1 878 6507
http://www.veritas.ie

CAFOD

Catholic Fund for Overseas Development,
Romero Close, Stockwell Road,
London SW9 8TY, U.K.

Tel: +44 171 733 7900
Fax: +44 171 274 9630
e-mail: hqcafod@cafod.org.uk
http://www.cafod.org.uk

SCIAF

Scottish Catholic International
Aid Fund (SCIAF),
19 Park Circus, Glasgow G3 6BE,
Scotland.

Tel: +44 141 354 5555
Fax: +44 141 354 5533
e-mail: sciaf@sciaf.org.uk
http://www.sciaf.org.uk

The opinions expressed are the author's and do not necessarily coincide with those of Trócaire, Veritas, Cafod or SCIAF.

Trócaire Editor: Maura Leen

Printed in Ireland by Genprint

ISBN 1 85390 537 2

Contents

Foreword
Bishop John Kirby, Chairman of Trócaire

World leaders have just held a special millennium summit to mark the year 2000. Many tasks await their urgent attention in this special Jubilee year. None is more pressing and more challenging than ensuring that the rights of refugees and forcibly displaced persons are protected and respected, and that the abuses of human rights, of which each refugee is a tragic symbol, are ended. That the scandal of 50 million people being forced to flee their homes, communities and often their families has followed us into this century is an indictment of our lack of response to the plight of this group and a denial of our common humanity. In a European context this is particularly disappointing as the 1951 UN Convention on Refugees arose out of the ashes of the Second World War and the huge refugee/displaced population in Europe at that time.

As the vast majority of refugees and forcibly displaced people remain in the developing world their plight may appear quite distant from us. But, as the experience of asylum seekers and refugees in Ireland and in other parts of Europe has shown, their treatment in seeking asylum on our shores has often been negative. While many communities have responded positively to asylum seekers and refugees, in line with Christ's social teaching on welcoming the newcomer in our midst, which is summed up in the powerful passage from the Gospel of St.Matthew " *I was a Stranger and You Welcomed Me*", (Mt. 25:35), others have not. Indeed in some cases a climate of fear and xenophobia has led to attacks on this already vulnerable group.

Much has been written on the asylum issue in Ireland. As a contribution to wider international debates on forced migration this booklet sets out the global situation of refugees and displaced persons, the root causes of the refugee phenomenon, the differing responses to it and the challenges we face both as individual members of society and as policymakers. In our daily work in the developing world, Trócaire, CAFOD and SCIAF are aware of the causes and consequences of refugee flows. Many of our partners have been victims of human rights abuses or have, as a result of threats, found themselves living in exile. A number of these people spoke about their experiences at Trócaire's special 25th anniversary conference in February 1998. Those who have returned home are now working to build a culture of peace and human rights in their home countries and to help end the cultures of impunity which forced them to flee in the first place.

This booklet is a rich resource in terms of analysis and reflection, as well as a restatement of the Christian commitment to solidarity and oneness of the human family as these relate to refugee issues. Its publication on the eve of the 50th anniversary of the establishment of UNHCR in December 1950 is timely. We are particularly pleased to have Mark Raper SJ and Amaya Valcárcel of Jesuit Refugee Service as authors of this book. Our agencies have worked with JRS in many countries. Current co-operation includes work with East Timorese refugees in West Timor and refugees along the Burmese border. Trócaire and CAFOD are also pleased that our sister organisation in Scotland, SCIAF (the Scottish Catholic International Aid Fund) has joined us as a co-publisher of the series.

Trócaire, CAFOD, and now SCIAF, owe a debt of profound gratitude to Professor Enda McDonagh, for his inspiring guidance for this booklet. I am confident that it will be of great practical use to our agencies in our involvement in policies and programmes which affect refugees and forcibly displaced persons.

I am also hopeful that the voices of refugees interspersed throughout the text will be read with interest and acted on by those charged with overseeing refugee policies here at home and at an international level.

A world suffused by the Christian commitment to the dignity of each and every person would be one where no one would be forced to flee his or her home. In the meantime, while actively pursuing this ideal world, we must at least ensure that those forced to flee are provided with a place of sanctuary, where they can feel safe and rebuild their lives in a spirit of hope. This booklet can guide us in this path.

Why don't you go back?

...Understand that it is not simple, nor easy,
avoiding past memory.
I can't remove from my mind
my traditional culture,
my sentimental torture,
the folktales of my childhood,
never old, never dead,
stamped in my mind.
I have normal feelings,
I suffer for dignity.
Please do not kill my broken heart...

Yilma Tafere, Ethiopia,
(Refugee Participation Network, September 1996)

ntroduction
Enda McDonagh, Series Editor

In 1998, as part of the celebrations of the 25th anniversary of its foundation and more importantly in preparation for its work in the new millennium, Trócaire began a fresh examination of its Christian-Catholic roots. Last year we were delighted to be joined in this by our sister organisation in England and Wales CAFOD, and this year we are pleased that our Scottish sister organisation SCIAF has joined us in co-publishing this series.

The aim of all these studies is to set in dialogue the rich and varied Christian tradition in teaching and practice of commitment to the poor and excluded with current concerns of development agencies like Trócaire, CAFOD, and SCIAF. In this way it is hoped to enlighten the Christian understanding and renew the spiritual energies of Trócaire, CAFOD and SCIAF, and their staff at home and abroad, and of their supporters and contributors. Without such enlightenment and renewal our vision and work could become narrow and frustrating.

The existing titles in the series, *Human Rights, Land, Famine* and *Food,* illustrated four of the most urgent concerns for development agencies. In seeking to expose Christian perspectives on these issues, the authors undertook a practical theological exploration from biblical background to contemporary analysis. While maintaining close communication with concrete problems of the day they have drawn on developing Christian tradition to illuminate and deepen commitment to justice in the world, the constituent element of the Gospel as the 1971 Synod of Bishops called it.

The series has already made a valuable contribution to that enlightenment and commitment both directly for individual readers and as the basis for seminars and study groups. The four volumes have been particularly helpful as resource books for our partners at home and abroad. By strengthening and further exploring the ethical dimensions of our work the series has enhanced our campaigning and education on justice and development issues. The series has been timely. The Jubilee 2000 campaign for debt cancellation, which has been particularly active in both Ireland and Britain, has illustrated the power of bringing ethics and values into policies that otherwise risk being pursued in a purely self-interested way.

The series is designed not only to enhance the understanding and motivation of development agencies and workers; the studies themselves make clear how much theology has to learn from work in the field, how much theory has to gain from praxis. In fact the social encyclicals which form the basis of so much social thought and activity in the Church were themselves influenced at various times by practical developments, as individual Church people and organisations reached out to the needy and excluded. In an increasingly pragmatic culture, the witness of Christian practice can be an effective way of understanding and expressing the presence of God. To do justice, the prophet Jeremiah says, is to know God. Engagement with the task of promoting a truly just world is for Christians a response to the call of the Reign or Kingdom of God. In the doing comes the understanding. Theologians need to learn by doing also and by being actively associated with the doers and seekers of justice, freedom, truth and peace.

Studies such as these will, it is hoped, prove of help to religious thinkers who have not yet had the opportunity for more active involvement in justice issues. Being drawn into that work, their insights into the whole range of Christian doctrine and practice, from the Trinity, Incarnation and the last things to environmental protection, will be undoubtedly enriched. Out of that enrichment they will contribute in turn to the Christian perspectives on development work that Trócaire, CAFOD and SCIAF are in search of here.

This volume on *Refugees and Forcibly Displaced People* tackles one of the developing world's most critical issues; an issue indeed which has already become a global one affecting immediately and sharply the host countries of our own and other agencies. Again the strategy of constructing a dialogue between the biblical / Christian tradition and the concrete reality of the refugee phenomenon is adopted. In the history of God's first people, Israel, and in that of the community of Jesus disciples there is much to be learned about the human plight of refugees escaping famine, poverty, war and persecution. There is even more to be learned from the divine call for hospitality to the homeless, the strangers in a foreign land who are particularly a manifestation of Christ who had nowhere to lay his head. It is by their response to these least ones, the hungry and homeless, that Christians will finally be judged.

Based on the worldwide and lengthy experience of the Jesuit Refugee Service, together with that of others committed to a sustained and structured response to this harrowing and growing human disaster, the authors of this booklet enlarge our Christian understanding. No longer will the readers be able to say "but we never saw You (Jesus) hungry or in exile or in a refugee camp". To escape the dread dismissal "Depart from me" the readers must follow that enlarged understanding with a more serious commitment to relieving the pressures that produce refugees and to welcoming effectively those who seek sanctuary. It is a long and daunting task, but Christ who is with them will also be with us as we reach out to them.

For Trócaire, CAFOD, SCIAF and other agencies multiple and diverse challenges remain, calling for systematic Christian reflection as well as sustained Christian commitment. Such reflections will feature in forthcoming volumes on AIDS and on Globalisation and a Global Ethic. So many topics will still demand Christian analysis and reflection that this series can only hope to stimulate others to pursue further theological tasks, formally or informally, in the years ahead.

As with any studies there are some dangers in doing such a series. There is the danger that such studies may become too self-enclosing or too bland or too negatively disputatious. With a good advisory team these particular dangers have been and continue to be averted. So can the more subtle one whereby the work of a development agency of explicit Christian Catholic inspiration is perceived as and/or becomes a vehicle for religious conversion.

Trócaire, CAFOD, and SCIAF have, true to their mandate and to their genuine Christian inspiration, respected these distinctions very scrupulously. It would be very sad if their attempt to explore their theological roots were to obscure rather than clarify their integrity as development agencies devoted fully to the personal and social needs of the people they serve without any threat to the cultural or religious integrity of these people. It will therefore continue to be a matter of real concern for the editor and authors of these studies to ensure that the renewal of Christian understanding and inspiration further protects and deepens the integrity of Trócaire, CAFOD and SCIAF and their work. In that also they will be making a further contribution to maintaining the varied vocation and work of the whole Church in the modern world.

xecutive Summary

Worldwide, every 21 seconds a refugee is created. Over the past decade the number of refugees and forcibly displaced persons has increased to the shocking figure of 50 million. While 5% of refugees seek sanctuary in Europe, over 90% remain in developing countries, and the majority are found in the poorest and least developed countries of sub-Saharan Africa. That this situation should exist at the dawn of a new millennium is an affront to our common humanity and evidence of a lack of effective global and national strategies to confront and tackle the violations of human rights which give rise to forced displacement in the first place.

This booklet, in setting out the issues both in political, developmental and ethical terms, seeks to inform the reader about the challenges we face as individuals, as Christians and as advocates for justice. While emphasising the vulnerability of refugees, the authors also point out that refugees and forcibly displaced people can, if given the chance, contribute greatly to their host societies with their skills, experience and energy, while adding to cultural diversity.

In "The State of the World's Refugees 1997-8 Report", UN Commissioner for Refugees, Sadako Ogata, wrote,

> "as human beings we have a responsibility to safeguard the security of all people. At the threshold of the 21st century, we are faced with the challenge to assure the universal protection of people by reinforcing even more than before the bonds of human compassion and solidarity. We yearn for the day when people in every part of the world can live safely within their own country and community."

Taking on the challenges set out in this booklet would go a long way to helping us reach that day.

Part one looks at the world we live in and the worldwide phenomenon of forced population movements. The situation of the displaced is examined by continent, with case examples from various countries used to illustrate wider trends. The different interpretation of who qualifies as a refugee, depending on where one finds oneself in the world, is highlighted. African and Latin American nations have more generous definitions of who is a refugee than Europe while a number of Asian states are still not even party to the 1951 Convention relating to the Status of Refugees.

Part one also includes an analysis of the root causes of forced migration and the complex interlinkages between these. The multidimensional nature of these causes necessities a multi-pronged approach to their solution. However, the fundamental unifying cause of forcible displacement remains the massive violations of human rights which persist in our world. Many of these violations occur in situations of armed conflicts, and many of these conflicts have their roots in poverty and the battle for resources. Undoubtedly, without concerted action to tackle poverty and inequality, conflicts will continue, and sadly, forcible displacement will remain the harsh reality for many.

Part one also provides an explanation of different categories of displaced persons, e.g. those living in refugee camps or those seeking asylum in third world countries, and their differing experiences. A particularly vulnerable group who fall outside the responsibility of the UNHCR (Office of the United Nations High Commissioner for Refugees) and which has grown rapidly during the 1990s, as internal or intra-state conflicts escalated, is that of internally displaced persons.

The final chapter of part one provides a gender perspective on the issues being examined. The majority of refugees and displaced persons are women and children in their care. This section brings us the voices and testimonies of women in exile and suggests gender sensitive responses aimed at respecting their rights, providing safety and protection, assisting integration into their host societies and helping them to rebuild their fractured lives.

Part two outlines what taking a Christian response would look like. It begins by noting that as Christians and as human beings we are one family travelling together and we share a common duty to welcome and accompany each other in our journey. Chapter six sets out the ingredients of what would constitute a truly Christian welcome to refugees and displaced people. Chapter seven outlines some pastoral challenges and emphasises how refugees show us to be true Christians and indeed enable us to understand and live our faith. At the same time, the authors are aware of the need to support the host communities in their efforts to welcome those arriving as strangers in their midst.

Other challenges which are discussed include reasserting the principle of *non-refoulement,* defending human rights, ending xenophobia, and stopping the influence and spread of restrictive western policies on refugees and asylum. That the world's richest nations should be adopting such restrictive practices as we approach the 50th anniversary of the 1951 UN Convention is particularly worrisome.

The booklet highlights, with examples from refugee practice, that without a fair asylum procedure we will compound the denial of basic rights experienced by refugees: first of all being forced to flee one's country and then only to find a resistance in the host country to the provision of such rights, as asylum (Article 14.1 of the 1948 Universal Declaration of Human Rights –UDHR - states that *everyone has the right to seek and to enjoy asylum from persecution)* and the right to a standard of living adequate for their well-being (Article 25 of UDHR).

The authors stress that change must take place at both personal and political levels. The field experience of Jesuit Refugee Service provides ample evidence in support of this view. This happens by listening to the stories of refugees and asylum seekers, by welcoming them into our churches, our communities, and by celebrating rather than fearing the cultural diversity which their arrival brings. To avoid becoming part of a fortress Europe or fortress Africa we need to break down attitudinal barriers to those whom we perceive to the different from ourselves. As the evidence provided in the book illustrates, the biggest barriers to refugees and displaced persons can be in our minds. Sometimes these are the hardest barriers to dismantle.   In tackling this, human rights education is vitally important. Indeed UN High Commissioner for Human Rights, Mary Robinson, has identified human rights education as the fourth "R" along with reading, writing and arithmetic.

As we start out on a new century, as part of a global community, we must ask ourselves what kind of world we want for this twenty-first century?   A key challenge is to build one where human rights are fully respected and the values of multiculturalism and inclusion are recognised and practiced. If we achieve this we shall not only have a better world for the refugee - we shall also have a better world for ourselves.

PART 1 THE WORLD WE LIVE IN

CHAPTER 1

Introduction

"I was a Stranger and You Welcomed Me" (Mt 25:35)

A millennium with 50 million forcibly displaced persons

UNHCR estimates for 1999 show that about 50 million people worldwide have been forcibly displaced from their homes. This number includes refugees, asylum seekers, returning refugees, and an estimated 30 million internally displaced persons. To put it differently, as we entered this millennium one in every 120 people on earth has been, forced to flee their home. Nearly 20 years ago, the Holy Father, Pope John Paul II, did not overstate the matter when he claimed: *"Of all the human tragedies of our day, perhaps the greatest is that of the refugees".*[1] He has also highlighted that the suffering of refugees is a *"shameful wound of our time"*, and *" a wound which typifies and reveals the imbalance and conflicts of the modern world".*[2]

Fifty years ago in 1950 those who gathered to set up the office of UNHCR and who formulated the 1951 UN Convention Relating to the Status of Refugees (Box 1) would have hoped that the services of this body would not be so much in demand today. Over the intervening years both UNHCR and the 1951 Convention have been the cornerstones of the international refugee protection regime. 137 countries are party to the Refugee Convention and/ or to the 1967 Protocol and the UNHCR is the leading international refugee agency.

---

[1] Speaking with refugees at Morong Camp, the Philippines, February 1981.
[2] Sollicitudo *Rei Socialis*, 1987, # 24.

Box 1 The 1951 Convention and its regional variants

The **1951 Convention relating to the Status of Refugees** defines a refugee as any person who, "owing to well-founded fear of being persecuted for reasons of race, religion, nationality, membership of a particular social group or political opinion, is outside the country of her/his nationality and is unable or, owing to such fear, is unwilling to avail him/herself of the protection of that country; or who, not having a nationality and being outside the country of her/his former habitual residence as a result of such events, is unable or, owing to such fear, is unwilling to return to it".

A basic principle, established in article 33 of the 1951 Convention, is the **principle of non-refoulement**, which is part of customary law, and as such all States must respect it, even if they are not party to the 1951 Convention. The article states:

> "No Contracting State shall expel or return ("refouler") a refugee in any manner whatsoever to the frontiers or territories where his/her life or freedom would be threatened on account of his/her race, religion, nationality, membership of a particular social group or political opinion."

Later, several regional treaties included language that broadened the 1951 Convention's definition of a refugee. The **OAU (Organisation of African Unity) Convention Governing the Specific Aspects of Refugee Problems in Africa**, adopted in 1969, repeats the definition found in the 1951 Convention, but also includes any persons compelled to leave their country "owing to external aggression, occupation, foreign domination or events seriously disturbing public order in either part of or the whole of his/her country of origin or nationality". ·

In 1984, a group of government representatives, academics and lawyers from Latin America met in Cartagena, Colombia, and adopted what became known as the **Cartagena Declaration**. Among other things, the Declaration recommended that the definition of a refugee used in the region should include, in addition to those fitting the 1951 Convention definition, persons who flee their country "because their lives, safety or freedom have been threatened by generalised violence, foreign aggression, internal conflicts, massive violation of human rights or other circumstances which have seriously disturbed public order".

Some of the instruments which protect refugees include: International Covenant on Civil Political Rights (1966); International Covenant on Economic Social Cultural Rights (1966); UN Convention on Elimination of All Forms of Discrimination Against Women (1979); UN Convention against Torture (1984, art.3); UN Convention on the Rights of the Child (1989); UN Declaration on the Protection of All Persons from Enforced Disappearance (1992).

However, the narrowness of the definition of refugees set out in the 1951 Convention quickly became apparent. In the 1950s, the term refugee had once more come to mean, as in the 1920s, refugee from communism. In practice, individual fear of persecution was not assessed for such persons. Asylum was virtually guaranteed in the West. The problem was getting out of the Warsaw Pact states. Exit visas for Soviet Jews and ethnic Germans became a major bargaining counter in East-West negotiations. By the time of the 1967 Protocol, however, the situation had changed dramatically. The wave of conflicts in the developing world gave rise to a new set of forced migrants, clearly deserving of international protection, but scarcely able to prove individual persecution, and much less welcome in the wealthier states of the so called 'developed world'.[3]

The complexity of refugee problems is illustrated by the expanding terminology which we use. We now distinguish between asylum seekers, stateless persons, illegal immigrants and undocumented persons. We also speak of mass expulsions, ethnic cleansing, forced migration, internal displacement, involuntary repatriation and imposed return. Determining who gains official refugee status has also become more and more complex. A person who is automatically recognised as a refugee in Africa may be no more than an asylum seeker in Europe. The 1951 Refugee Convention is being interpreted more restrictively. Thankfully the OAU (Africa) and Cartagena (Latin America) Conventions are broader and more suited to contemporary conditions (see Box 1). Some countries have argued that the 1951 Refugee Convention is no longer relevant to contemporary forms of conflict and displacement. Admittedly, many of those who use this argument (including western European states) are also the worst offenders when it comes to compliance. There is a strong argument, however, that if the Refugee Convention

---

[3] Mark Leopold and Barbara Harell-Bond, "An Overview of the World Refugee Crisis", 1997.

were to be re-written, it would result in far weaker protection for refugees.

Ironically, the world should be a more peaceful place. The Cold War is over. Conflicts between sovereign states are few. Regional conflicts like those once witnessed in Indochina, Southern Africa, and Central America are no longer fanned into flames by super-power conflicts. And a global nuclear meltdown seems unlikely — despite some recent nuclear muscle flexing on the Indian subcontinent. Yet paradoxically, intense new conflicts are breaking out almost uncontrollably within national borders. In 9 cases out of 10, the victims of such conflicts are civilians. All these conflicts displace people. Ninety percent of those displaced come from the world's least developed regions. Even when, as fugitives, they manage to cross borders, nearly all remain within the world's least developed regions. Yet while conflicts have a local dimension, many of their causes are global in origin, for instance unequal access to resources or external support for undemocratic governments. A huge international trade in arms also fuels such conflicts.

The global environment for the world's refugees is not good. Refugees no longer hold the political or strategic currency that they did during the Cold War period. States no longer have a strategic interest in hosting refugees, and generous refugee policies rarely win popular votes in countries with growing unemployment and competing domestic demands and tensions. In a trend set largely in the industrialised North (Western Europe and North America), countries are closing their doors to refugees and asylum seekers, and erecting increasingly elaborate barriers and restrictions for those seeking to enter their territories, including spurious interpretations of the refugee definition and restrictive applications of its provisions.

Global economic crises have meant that the distinction between economic migrants and refugees has become ever more blurred, and host governments' immigration and asylum policies are frequently influenced more by a desire to protect themselves and keep people out, than to provide protection to others. Thus international refugee protection is under threat and the rights of refugees and asylum seekers are being eroded. In Western Europe, for example, only 8.5% of asylum seekers in 1998 were awarded full Convention refugee status along with the other rights it confers. Instead, countries have sometimes opted to grant a temporary form of protection with limited rights and benefits.

Added to this is the problem that 50 years after its adoption, unlike many of the other international human rights instruments, there is still no independent body to monitor state compliance with the 1951 Refugee Convention. Although people have suggested that UNHCR is the appropriate guardian of the 1951 Convention, others, including Amnesty International, have argued that as an inter-governmental body which is paid and managed by states and which is directly responsible for providing protection and assistance to refugees, UNHCR does not have the independence to fulfil this role. As a result, states circumvent their obligations under the Convention with almost total impunity. Meanwhile, in large sections of the world, most notably in Asia, many states have still not ratified the Refugee Convention and neither are they bound by any national or regional refugee laws.

Displacement – A Worldwide Phenomenon

Continental Trends

Every continent and every region of the world is affected by the problem of forced displacement. Whole generations of people in Africa, the Middle East and Asia have known no other life than that lived in a refugee camp. Denied education, children lose their hope in the future. Adults lose their roles, their skills and their dignity. Communities become dependent and cultures are atrophied. Lost generations linger in legal, social and political limbo, often ignored by the international community. When not ignored, the lives of refugees risk distortion in the high profile crises that draw the media's attention. But in all those conflicts that have reached our TV screens in recent years, whether in Rwanda, Kosovo, East Timor, Angola, Colombia, Sierra Leone, Burundi or Chechnya, the real story of these crises can be, read in the faces of the refugees they create and can be heard in their voices.

J.K., a Rwandan refugee, points out:

> " I belong to a lost generation, like all people of my age, who have been displaced since October 1990 by the war, and without a country since the bloody spring of 1994. My brother and sister should have been attending high school now, soon to take off with their own wings. Today, they are still at starting of point. There is no chance now for them to make their dreams come true. They also form part of a lost generation. My cousin was studying medicine. Today, his name should feature in prestigious lists of eminent doctors. But these intellectual capacities have been frozen because he lives in a refugee camp. Another member of a lost generation. Many of our youth have also been lost, because of tough conditions they face living in exile

which prompt promiscuity. All this must stop. It is too much. The international community must be made aware of the level of destruction in Rwandan society. No one can be proud of what happened, even those who won."

(J.K. a Rwandan refugee)

Africa

"Padiri (Father), I thank God for three things. First, because after waiting three years, the Lord has given me what I desired so much: a son and a daughter. Second, after the death of my husband, I felt exhausted, without strength to undertake this long path of exile towards the unknown, with these two young children. But after having walked a long time along the road, a car stopped and took us to Bukavu. Finally, when we arrived to Bukavu, I had the chance to meet a sister who worked in the city's hospital. My husband died of AIDS. Thanks to this sister, I was able to do the tests to see whether my children were infected. You could never imagine the joy I felt when I knew they were not infected with the virus; however, I am HIV positive myself."

(Emma, a Rwandan refugee in the Bukavu camps, Congo-Zaire, 1996, speaks to Quim Pons SJ)

Africa is the main refugee-generating and refugee-hosting continent. Political and ethnic conflicts in the Great Lakes region, which includes Burundi, Rwanda and the Democratic Republic of Congo, have generated millions of refugees in the past decade alone. Most of these who are displaced remain within the region, even within the refugee-generating countries themselves, as well as in Tanzania, Uganda, Kenya and Zambia. The upheaval in Congo-Brazzaville, although largely unnoticed and not much examined in Western newspapers, has nonetheless uprooted over half a million people.

The Horn of Africa has also witnessed continual armed conflicts which have provoked millions to flee in search of safety. The conflict in southern Sudan has displaced over 4 million people. The struggle for Eritrean independence from Ethiopia lasted practically 40 years. Yet just this year the world witnessed former allies engaged in a bloody fratricide in which thousands have been slaughtered. Somalia remains fractured since the collapse of the artificially propped-up dictatorship of Siad Barre. Most of the refugees from these conflicts now live in Uganda, Kenya or Egypt.

In Southern Africa, Mozambique is still absorbing the millions of refugees, demobilised soldiers and internally displaced persons who returned home after years of war. Despite floods, a recent cyclone and bitterly contested elections, there is increasing freedom and a steadily growing economy. Yet this growth is not able to deliver on poverty reduction to the extent required as the country still carries a heavy burden of external debt.

Angola should have been set on the same path after its 1994 peace accord. Instead it has been plunged back into a war fuelled by the mineral wealth of the country, the folly of the international community that allows these minerals to be traded for weapons, and the greed of its own leaders. Three and a half million Angolans are now displaced within their country and new refugees arrive daily from Angola into Zambia, Namibia and Congo. The southern Africa region is also home to a large number of urban refugees – now a phenomenon in most African cities. Urban refugees are those who either do not have access to other means of survival or who do not accept the dubious privilege of living on rations in a remote refugee camp. They drift to the cities to earn a living under conditions of greater anonymity. The picture is no better in West Africa. In this region civil wars in Liberia and Sierra

Leone have left thousands of their citizens in neighbouring countries, afraid to return to their original lands.

Asia and the Middle East

"Please God it (my visit) will help to draw attention to your continuing plight. You have been deprived of many things, which represent basic needs of the human person: proper housing, health care, education and work. Above all, you bear the sad memory of what you were forced to leave behind, not just material possessions, but your freedom, the closeness of relatives, and the familiar surroundings and cultural traditions which nourished your personal and family life."

(Pope John Paul II addressing Palestinian refugees, March 2000)

Palestinian refugees in the Middle East and Burmese ethnic minorities living in Thailand compete to be the longest running refugee populations in the world. Each group has its origins in the 1940s or earlier. The conflict over Kashmir also dates from the time of the partition of India and Pakistan, as does the displacement of the so-called 'Bihari Muslims', an Urdu speaking minority within Bangladesh. When the Soviet Union pushed down into Afghanistan in 1979 it began a conflict that has displaced millions of people, the majority of whom have fled to Pakistan and Iran. Despite the withdrawal of the Soviet Union and indeed its own collapse, the violence initiated over 20 years ago has hardly abated.

The plight of Tibetan refugees following the occupation of Tibet by China is a well known refugee tragedy, thanks to their widely respected spiritual leader, the Dali Lama, publicising their case. But largely unknown is the fate of 100,000 Bhutanese, only marginally less than the numbers of Tibetans who fled, who have been rendered stateless and for 10 years have been confined to camps in the lowland region of Nepal.

One of the most poignant of today's conflicts is taking place in Sri Lanka. This conflict has produced a worldwide diaspora which rivals that of the Sudanese. While seemingly the result of ethnic divisions the conflict, like so many others, is about power and control. 100,000 Sri Lankan Tamil refugees live in Southern India, many of them in small camps, which the United Nations has been asked to help but to which it is denied access, since India along with all but a handful of Asian nations, has still not signed the 1951 Refugee Convention.

Joel Kulanayagem SJ and Alfred Gabriel SJ, JRS workers, capture the plight of those affected by the conflict in the rebel-held areas of Sri Lanka when they write:

> "The constant conflict has multiplied the already severe hardships faced by the people. An economic embargo is in force in the northern and eastern provinces of Sri Lanka where the indigenous Tamils settled as a majority since the outbreak of war. The full impact of the embargo is felt by innocent civilians rather than militants. Far from succumbing, the militants have become stronger over the years. Also, the embargo has made many civilians, be they Sinhalese, Muslim or Tamil, and many security personnel rich through bribery and corruption. It is the ordinary civilian in the Vanni who has to suffer the inhuman economic embargo, and s/he has been suffering for years (…) Available food stocks have been dwindling fast and prices are shooting up. Shops are emptying, bakers have stopped operating, and bread has disappeared. Even for a cup of tea or coffee, sugar is hardly available. Hospitals and medical clinics are running out of medicines. Postal services have come to a standstill. Banks cannot cope with the demands of their customers; liquid cash is becoming a serious problem since the government does not allow money into the Vanni."

In south east Asia, twenty five years after the ending of the Vietnam War and the "side-show" conflicts which it provoked in Cambodia and Laos, the last of the Lao refugees have just either returned home or been resettled. Disputes arise still over the safety of new Cambodian refugees in Thailand, and pockets of Vietnamese remain detained in Thailand or without full rights of residence in Hong Kong. Worldwide sympathy, which overflowed towards the Indo-Chinese refugees in a former era, has now frozen solid. Elsewhere, for over two decades, the people of East Timor have suffered the pragmatic silence of the world in the face of Indonesia's attempt to swallow the territory. Standing in the ruins of their houses, without work, without shelter, the Timorese can for the moment smile, because they are free. The enormous challenge of nation building and enabling refugees to return home now lies ahead of them.

The Americas

While the Cold War has ended, the oppression and displacement of indigenous minorities in many countries, for example in Chiapas in Mexico, and the violence associated with large scale, poverty-induced labour migrations have not yet been eliminated. "Undocumented" Haitians who live and work effectively as slaves in the Dominican Republic are examples of such migrants. In Colombia, rural peasants are caught in the middle of the conflict between military, paramilitary (the security forces protecting commercial interests) and guerrilla forces. Described by North and South American groups as "our hemisphere's most serious humanitarian crisis", over a million people have been forcibly displaced in their own country by this competition for land and power. The United States, in a massive plan supposedly aimed at imposing peace, is proposing to fund the Colombian military, one of the main culprits wreaking violence on the Colombian people, and equip it with weapons. Far from building peace and tackling the drug problem, this *Plan Colombia* will entrench and exacerbate conflict and with it human suffering.

Europe

> *"Much of the problem comes from one simple fact: we don't believe refugees...In other words, the "culture of disbelief" can make us deaf to genuine cries for protection. We must allow their cries of pain to be heard."*

(Lena Barrett, JRS Europe Policy and Information officer)

One of the most dramatic, man-made crises of forced displacement today results from the brutal and unchallenged war in Chechnya. The rest of the world both needs and fears the Russian State and thus will not openly challenge its actions. Other countries of the former Soviet Union also receive and repel refugees. In recent years all eyes have been turned towards south-eastern Europe, most especially when the NATO bombing of Serbia began in March 1999 and two million Albanian Kosovars were displaced, over 800,000 of them into the neighbouring countries, especially Macedonia, Albania and Montenegro. Bosnia lives under an imposed and uneasy peace. Reconciliation is at least a generation away.

As the borders of Western Europe are increasingly being closed off to many immigrants and asylum seekers, the problem is being pushed further East. Poland, Hungary, Czech Republic, Romania and Lithuania all receive Sri Lankans, Sudanese, Afghans, many seeking work, many seeking safety, most seeking to go further west. Everywhere, but especially in Europe, the task of distinguishing refugees from ordinary migrants presents new and serious difficulties. Formerly migration and refugee movements were discrete phenomena. Refugees could be distinguished from 'economic migrants' whose claims were regarded as 'fake'. But now it has become increasingly difficult to distinguish between 'voluntary' and 'involuntary' population movements, between people who are fleeing from threats to their life and those seeking to escape poverty and social injustice.

For the refugee there is an intensifying experience of rejection, what Professor James C. Hathaway has termed 'politics of non-*entrée*'[4]. The aim of many countries' is containment: to keep refugees at a distance. The unpopularity of migrants is tangible. Sophisticated mechanisms are being upgraded to keep newcomers out of zones of prosperity. The creation of 'safe havens', re-admission agreements, temporary protective status, safe third country lists, summary exclusion procedures at airports, the removal of social benefits for asylum seekers, and the push for repatriation are all instruments of containment. The media, too, are enlisted to protect us from the forcibly displaced, ignoring their sufferings and oversimplifying their struggles. Restrictive legislation on immigration, ungenerous policies regarding asylum requests and the upsurge of extremist anti-foreigner groups all typify western European trends.

On the positive side, harmonisation of asylum and immigration policies will at least set minimum standards. Many EU countries have had or are thinking of having regularisations of migrants, which should ease the hardship faced by rejected asylum seekers who cannot be expelled. But the closure of borders to prevent unwanted refugee influxes is not only a Western phenomenon. Even a country like Tanzania, which had a previously admirable record of admitting refugees, has done so. And the sacred principle of voluntary repatriation is being over-ridden: 20 countries expelled refugees from their territories during 1996.

---

[4] Prof. James C. Hathaway, *The Law of Refugee Status,* Butterworths, Canada, 1991.

Asia - Who protects refugees?

In Asia, two factors - globalisation and rising fundamentalism - are at the root of new and often violent conflicts. Because of the rapid changes taking place in traditional societies due to globalisation, people feel a sense of confusion, and therefore yearn to return to the old way of life, thus paving the way for fundamentalism to grow. Division and forced segregation of people according to religion, language, culture and caste have resulted in much bloodshed, loss of life and damage to property. In all these situations, the unfortunate victims are the poor and marginalised.

Unlike Africa or America, Asia has no regional refugee definition to guide its policies and practices, but operates (where refugee status is recognised at all) on the most restricted definitions. Michael Alexander, a former JRS Policy Officer in the Asia Pacific region, explains how refugees are treated in this region. He said that in most of the countries of Asia, and in other parts of the world, refugee status determination is conducted not by governments but by UNHCR. For the most part asylum-seekers have no choice but to approach UNHCR, because very few governments in the region are parties to the 1951 Convention relating to the Status of Refugees and its 1967 Protocol. Even some of those countries which are parties (e.g. Cambodia) do not have their own refugee status determination processes, so refugees cannot apply directly to those governments for recognition. UNHCR steps in to fill the gap. UNHCR carries out this process pursuant to the mandate given in its statute to provide international protection to refugees.

Africa: Insecurity and exile

"When the rebels entered Sudan, we ran from Juba to Nimule. When I was in Nimule with my children, some people broke into my house. They started to beat me, a disabled woman. I left my husband in the town, I do not

*know where he is now. I have seven children and they are
suffering. I am finding difficulties to care for them, to
provide school fees, clothing, blankets and books. I also
came across two orphans, and it is not easy to help them."*

(Rebecca Ifuho, Rhino refugee camp settlement,
northern Uganda)

Since the late 1980s, there has been a marked shift in refugee
policies in Africa, which became particularly pronounced in
the 1990s. African states have become less committed to
providing asylum. Instead of opening their doors to persons
fearing persecution, African countries now prefer refugees to
receive protection in "safe zones" or similar areas within their
countries of origin. African states now routinely reject refugees
at their frontiers or return them to their countries of origin even
if the conditions from which they have fled still persist.
Refugees who manage to enter and remain in host countries
receive "pseudo-asylum". Their physical security, dignity and
material safety are not guaranteed. As for solutions, African
states are less inclined to grant local settlement or resettlement
opportunities to refugees. What they seem to prefer is
repatriation at the earliest opportunity, regardless of the
situation in the countries of origin.

There are several reasons that have led to this change of
policy:

i) The magnitude of the refugee problem,
In Africa, the refugee problem has grown both in magnitude
and complexity. In the Great Lakes, for example, there was an
influx of some 250,000 Rwandan refugees into Tanzania
within 24 hours in April 1994.

ii) Regional Insecurity
Some refugee hosting countries have encountered serious
external relations problems with the countries of origin, which

in some cases have led to armed conflagration. An example is the ongoing acrimonious fighting between Burundi and Tanzania, which arises out of Tanzania's decision to grant refuge to Burundi refugees fleeing from political violence. Thus when large numbers of people flee situations of conflict and grave human rights violations, their security and protection often remain at risk even when they reach places of refuge. The problem of security in refugee camps has received a great deal of international attention in recent years, largely, but not only, prompted by the ongoing refugee crisis in the Great Lakes region of Africa. The militarisation and non-civilian character of refugee camps; the use of camps as military training grounds; cross-border attacks and incursions; the forced conscription and abduction of children into armed forces; sexual and domestic violence against women; these are all problems that have been experienced in a number of countries including Tanzania, Guinea and Liberia.

The plight of those caught in these camps is described by a Rwandan refugee in Bukavu:

> "It took me time to get used to sleeping in a tent. After our long walk we were exhausted, but finally we arrived. Later, during the night, we were all suddenly awoken by a repetitive sound. We stayed there, under the sheeting. When we woke up the next morning, they told us that there were bombs in Birava. Since then, I have problems to sleep. My children call me during the night, they have difficulties sleeping too."

Measures which would improve protection and security include: moving camps a safe distance away from borders to prevent cross-border attacks; thoroughly screening refugee populations to ensure the civilian composition of camp populations; more rigorous application of the exclusion clauses under the 1951 Convention, which exclude certain categories of individuals (such as war criminals) from international protection; strengthening UNHCR's protection mandate; and improving the quality of protection provided through better training for UNHCR field staff, particularly in the area of human rights and humanitarian standards. At the same time concerns about security should not mean that refugee settlements are managed in a non-participatory, authoritarian manner.

iii) The impact of refugees on host countries

This includes damage to the environment, ecology and infrastructure. African countries resent the absence of meaningful burden-sharing for a problem which they perceive neither as their problem nor as one which they are able to bear alone. The restrictive policies currently employed in industrialised countries to keep out refugees have also led African states to take steps within their means to achieve the same ends. Most of the major refugee hosting countries in Africa are poor and highly indebted. They therefore need to be given international assistance and debts should be cancelled in order to provide them with the resources to support proper asylum services. The aid provided should be timely and adequate to meet the entitlements of refugees, particularly those relating to physical and material security including food, shelter, clothing and medical supplies.

iv) Growing xenophobia in many African countries.

Today's refugees come from independent African countries. Host populations do not have the same sympathy for them as they had for asylum seekers in the 1960s and 1970s who were fleeing from armed struggles against colonialism, racial domination and apartheid. Xenophobic sentiments have emerged at a time when most of Africa is democratising and governments are compelled to take into account public opinion in formulating their policies. The result has been the adoption of anti-refugee platforms by political parties, which result in anti-refugee policies and practices by governments. Therefore, efforts at public education and awareness need to be stepped up to educate populations about the special status of refugees and why, unlike other aliens, refugees need and deserve international protection. Such education and information campaigns should target all segments of African society.

The continued availability of asylum in Africa will depend on the problems that are currently preventing refugee policy formation from being addressed. Tackling the huge scale of the refugee problem also requires that the root causes of forced migration be addressed. These causes include poverty, conflicts (and the arms trades which fuel them), violations of human rights and the impunity granted to those who make it impossible for others to remain in their home countries.

The Americas: New forms of forced migration

"The guerrillas kidnapped me when they besieged my home village in 1999. The military barracks were destroyed, many people fled, shops and houses were looted. People in the village were so confused. There were different armed groups, all fighting one another. We don't even know who is who in this war. We don't know why they fight, or for what."

(Daniela, an asylum seeker from Colombia)

Peace agreements in Central America have ended a number of long running civil wars. However, they failed to deliver better life conditions for local people. In El Salvador, many of those who were repatriated under bilateral and regional agreements face continued persecution, including bombardment and armed attacks on returnee settlements. While signing accords means that peace is declared, to be sustainable peace needs to be built by creating or recreating a culture of human rights and non-violence.

Nowadays, in Latin America, forced migration and the violence linked to it defy conventional definitions. Our understanding of who is a refugee must be broad enough to include those whose lives are most precarious or those who would otherwise be forgotten. For example, the Haitian population in the Dominican Republic is extremely vulnerable. Forced to live in constant fear of expulsion, they do not enjoy the same rights as properly documented migrants and are subject to human rights violations and xenophobic attacks.

Yet in a climate of peace and human rights we should welcome forcibly displaced people, despite their precarious legal identity, or the fact that they may have been trafficked. Some years ago Pope John Paul gave a clear instruction in this regard:

> "The Church, as sacrament of unity...of the whole
> human race, is the locus where immigrants whose
> situation is illegal are also welcomed and recognised
> as brothers and sisters. The various dioceses have the
> duty to mobilise themselves so that these persons...
> may be welcomed as brothers and sisters in the
> Christian community."[5]

The most critical ongoing armed conflict in Latin America is the Colombian civil war. More than 1.2 million people have already been internally displaced, and more people continue to be displaced following frequent massacres, perpetrated by guerrillas, paramilitary groups and state actors. The complex causes of internal displacement in Colombia are described by Francis Deng and Roberta Cohen in their study, *The Forsaken People: Case Studies of the Internally Displaced*:

> "At the root of these problems, lie the enormous
> disparities in the distribution of land and wealth, a loss
> of legitimacy by the government, the crises affecting

---

[5] John Paul II, "Migrants and their Irregular Situation", May 1995.

and ineffectiveness of established institutions, an oligarchic political and social system based on clientelism, state use of terrorist methods, a breakdown of social relations, the lack of access to the organs of power for the majority of Colombians, the physical absence of the state in many regions, and a highly militarised society."

Detention of Asylum Seekers – the US experience

"As a refugee who spent two years and four months in Wackenhut Detention Centre in Queens before I was granted asylum, I know how important it is to have support from people who come to help keep hope alive. Refugees come to this country thinking it is a land of freedom - freedom of speech, freedom of religion, freedom from persecution-. Detention almost killed my soul. Prayer and humanity saved me."

(Adelaide Abankwah from Ghana, in a letter to the *New York Times*, February 2000)

In industrialised and developing countries alike, the detention of asylum seekers has become a common practice often used as a deterrent strategy to stem refugee flows. Asylum seekers are frequently detained, sometimes arbitrarily and indefinitely and without the right to judicial review. The detention of asylum seekers frequently obstructs their access to legal assistance and information and thus the right to a full and fair hearing of their asylum applications. Furthermore, detaining asylum seekers— many of whom may have escaped from countries where they have been imprisoned, tortured and ill-treated, have fled in fear and are severely disoriented—can have a serious impact on mental health. Incarceration, often in inhumane conditions, alongside prisoners with criminal convictions or those awaiting trial, or restrictions on freedom of movement is entirely inappropriate treatment for asylum seekers. Moreover, inhumane conditions of incarceration violate international standards on humane treatment in detention.

Human Rights Watch research shows that the U.S. Immigration and Naturalisation Service (INS) housed more than half of its 16,000 detainee asylum seekers in local jails throughout the country in 1998. The INS had failed to ensure that basic national and international standards requiring humane treatment and adequate conditions had been met. INS detainees were treated the same as local inmates, and jail staff were not trained in dealing with the special problems of asylum seekers and immigrants. Many INS detainees had been physically abused by jail staff. Medical and dental care was found to be substandard at many of the jails, and access for families, friends, and legal representatives was severely curtailed due to strict and inappropriate jail rules. Lack of access to legal representation, information, and assistance subsequently often had serious implications for the cases of asylum seekers and immigrants, and obstructed their right to a full and fair hearing.

Asylum seekers should not, as a general rule, be detained. The current French Presidency of the EU has stated that *"the detention of asylum seekers simply because they are asylum seekers should not occur"*. The right to seek and enjoy asylum is a basic human right, and individuals must never be punished for seeking asylum in the United States or elsewhere. Furthermore, the decision to detain an asylum seeker can be justified only when proven to be strictly necessary and even then only on a case-by-case basis. If detention does occur the conditions attached to it should at least reflect the non-accused, non-criminal status of all INS detainees. Immigrant detainees should therefore not be held in prisons or any other facility intended to house criminal populations or those accused of or charged with criminal offenses.

All possible alternatives to detention should be exhausted before any decision to detain is made. Such alternatives include unsupervised and supervised parole, bail and reporting systems. In cases where detention of asylum seekers is required, they should never be held in facilities where necessary access to legal counsel and other resources is severely hindered.

Europe: The experience of rejection

"Why are you here in Europe?" I asked. *"How many Tamils are there in Europe?"* he replied. *"About 24,000,"* I answered. *"Then there are about 24,000 reasons why I am here."*

The trends in European asylum policy reveal the growing unwillingness of states to adhere to their obligations under the 1951 Convention. An example of this attitude was the response of E.U. states to the arrival of several thousand Turkish and Iraqi Kurds in Italy in January 1998. Panic at what was perceived as a "mass influx" prompted the E.U. to adopt an "E.U. Action Plan on the Influx of Migrants from Iraq and the Neighbouring Region" of which Human Rights Watch was heavily critical.

A disturbing aspect is the trend away from providing full refugee status and instead replacing this with various forms of temporary protection. Temporary protection, which was always intended to be an exceptional measure to deal with mass influxes of refugees, as occurred during the crisis in the former Yugoslavia from 1992 onwards, is fast becoming the norm. During its presidency of the EU the then Austrian government proposed introducing a new temporary protection regime and a solidarity scheme for the reception of refugees in Europe which would supplement, amend, or replace the existing 1951 Convention. In so doing it argued that the Convention was no longer applicable to most asylum seekers coming to Europe.

This shift towards temporary protection may ultimately result in fewer rights for refugees, absolve governments of many of their international obligations, and shift the burden back to poorer developing countries which are least equipped to deal with large population influxes. After an outcry by UNHCR and NGOs, the other EU member states fairly speedily and outrightly rejected the Austrian Presidency's proposal. In the Tampere conclusions agreed during the Finnish Presidency of the EU (October 1999), the Council explicitly stated that the EU commits itself to a full and inclusive application of the 1951 Refugee Convention.

In 1999, the fifteen member States of the EU received roughly 360,000 applications for asylum. This represented an increase of just under 20% on the previous year, but it is still well below the peak of 700,000 applications received in 1992. This represented a small proportion of a global total of refugees and displaced persons numbering 50 million. However, European governments tend to look upon this so-called "influx" with a singularly jaundiced eye. They believe that most applicants are motivated not by a need to escape protection, but by the desire to improve their economic situation.

Refugees or Economic Migrants?

Some people choose to migrate, to start again in a new country, in the hope of a better future for themselves and their children. Others are forced to migrate; they have no choice, as they are in danger. They may have to leave everything behind, with little hope of ever regaining the social and economic status that they had in their home country. There are many cases of doctors, lawyers, journalists and other professionals who, faced with the language barrier, and non-recognition of their qualifications, are only able to find manual work in their host country. In between these two situations, there are others who are motivated by a tangled mixture of hopes and fears, anxious to leave an intolerable situation, hoping that life will be better elsewhere.

Asylum is designed to protect people who are forced out of their country by a well-founded fear of persecution; it is not meant to be a substitute for an immigration policy. Until Europe recognises its own need for migrants (which currently creates a steady demand for black market labour), and implements a realistic system for legal immigration, every asylum-seeker will continue to be an object of suspicion by the authorities, with dangerous consequences for those in need of protection.

Barriers to entry

Because refugees are seen as "bogus", measures are taken to prevent them getting into the host country. These measures affect everyone, no matter how serious a person's need for protection. Those fleeing persecution are required to produce a proper passport and visa - regardless of the fact that someone being targeted by his or her own state is going to have difficulty persuading that state to provide him or her with adequate documentation. Many are forced to pay substantial sums for fake documents, and risk being regarded as criminals as a result, with their asylum application deemed "manifestly unfounded".

Another reason why asylum applications are declared "manifestly unfounded", and therefore subjected to unsatisfactory accelerated procedures, is that the applicant is deemed to come from a safe country of origin. This is alarming: every individual should be able to have his or her case considered on its individual merits, not on the basis of preconceived ideas. If an individual faces persecution, it is hardly consoling to have one's application rejected on the basis that one's country is safe for most people. There is also a serious question to be raised about how a country is deemed safe: by whom, for whom, and on the basis of what information?

For those who succeed in entering a host country, further difficulties lie in store. They risk being taken into detention without warning, for uncertain periods, as frequently happens in the UK or Germany. There is a tendency for states to make social conditions for asylum seekers as unappealing as possible, in the hope of discouraging all but the most desperate: restricted access to work, the refusal to give cash payments, and forced dispersal away from potential social networks. Asylum interviews are often bruising experiences, during which the applicant feels that s/he is automatically disbelieved, and the interviewer is trying to trap her/him into contradicting her/himself. A study published by the Irish Refugee Council in September 2000 on asylum in Ireland found that the minimum legal standards laid down in international resolutions and agreements are not always adhered to by the Irish Department of Justice in the initial determination of asylum applications[6]. Because states are reluctant to believe asylum claims, the rates for granting refugee status are low, which in turn fuels the belief that most asylum applications are ungrounded, and so on into a vicious circle of disbelief.

European coordination

Member states want to control not only primary movements - people entering the EU - but secondary movements, that is where asylum applicants who move from one EU country to another to claim asylum. The Dublin Convention (currently under review by the European Commission) says that the first EU country where an individual has the chance to apply for asylum should be the country that determines that asylum

---

[6] *Asylum in Ireland,* Report of the Irish Refugee Council, 2000. This study makes 52 recommendations aimed at improving the assessment procedure and bringing it into line with the provisions of the various international instruments governing refugees, and with European standards to which Ireland has agreed. The motivation for the project came in part from the divergence in numbers between those granted refugee status at first instance, as opposed to at appeal. In 1998 only 6% were successful initially, but 38% succeeded on appeal. This divergence raised the question as to what was wrong with the initial procedure. See also report by Carol Coulter, *Irish Times*, September 8th, 2000.

claim. If asylum seekers move from one country to another, it is assumed that their claim must be weak, and that this is a strategy to stay in the EU as long as possible for economic reasons. However, this reasoning ignores the fact that conditions for refugees - both legal and social - vary so widely across Europe that finding protection can be like playing a lottery. After coming so far, and investing so much, it is entirely reasonable for refugees to look for the best prospects of safety. France and Germany, for example, refuse to believe that people can become refugees because they fear persecution by non-state actors such as armed opposition groups. For certain asylum-seekers these countries would truly not be safe places in which to seek asylum, as the English Court of Appeal recognised in 1999.

There are also differences in the social conditions faced by asylum-seekers; some states are more likely than others to detain applicants; some states grant residence permits to people who do not fulfil the 1951 Convention definition of a refugee, but whom for various reasons it would be inhumane to deport, while other states do not. There are also wide differences in the temporary protection regimes for people who are seen as needing short-term refuge - this is one reason why the response to the Kosovo crisis was so fragmented. States have an interest in making themselves as unattractive to asylum-seekers as possible, so that potential applicants go elsewhere: this leads in a destructive race to the bottom as far as legal and social standards are concerned. Recognising that this is unacceptable, the Amsterdam Treaty provides that EU states will work towards creating common standards for asylum-seekers. Everyone who needs protection should be guaranteed it no matter which EU country she or he arrives in.

Certain member States have also concluded bilateral arrangements with other European states outside the EU that they consider "safe third countries" (such as Germany's agreement with Poland) to allow asylum-seekers to be sent back there to have their claims considered. This places a heavy burden especially on Central and Eastern European states whose asylum systems are still in the formative stages. There is no proper tracking mechanism to follow what happens to asylum-seekers sent to a "safe third country", and there is a very real fear that some risk undergoing a series of chain deportations, and ultimately being sent back to the persecuting home country.

A more ambitious plan by the EU is to provide assistance to certain countries of origin of migrants and refugees, on the basis that, if the situation improved, then others would not need to leave. In 1999, the EU Council approved Plans of Action for five countries: Afghanistan, Iraq, Morocco, Somalia and Sri Lanka (Albania and surrounding regions will also be dealt with). The Action Plans have lofty aims ranging from preventing human rights abuses to promoting employment opportunities, but to date there has been a reluctance to decide exactly how these aims will be achieved, who will implement the various plans and where the money will come from. There is merit in principle in these initiatives as no one should be forced to leave his/her country. But there is a danger that pressure will be put on the countries covered by these plans to prevent their citizens from leaving, or that people will be returned prematurely, or that aid will be conditional on the prevention of migration. Assisting someone in his or her country of origin so that she or he does not have to leave is beneficial; forcing someone to stay in a persecuting state is not.

CHAPTER 3 The root causes of forced migration

In 1997, Pope John Paul II stated:

> "The Church looks with deep pastoral concern at the increased flow of migrants and refugees, and questions herself about the causes of this phenomenon and the particular conditions of those who are forced for various reasons to leave their homeland. In fact the situation of the world's migrants and refugees seems ever more precarious. Violence sometimes obliges entire populations to leave their homeland to escape repeated atrocities; more frequently, it is poverty and the lack of prospects for development which spur individuals and families to go into exile, to seek ways to survive in distant lands, where it is not easy to find a suitable welcome."

For many years the task of distinguishing refugees from ordinary migrants did not present serious difficulty to states. Migration and refugee flows were regarded as has already been indicated, discrete phenomena. As has already been indicated, it has now become increasingly difficult to make a clear distinction between "voluntary" and "involuntary" population movements, between people who are fleeing from threats to their life and those seeking to escape poverty and social injustice. There are in many countries extreme conditions in which the requirements of survival are not met. What moves people to seek a better life often includes the search for security from such a hostile environment that may not include "persecution" as such. Today, more than ever, refugees are part of a complex migratory phenomenon, in which political, ethnic, economic, environmental and human rights factors are all contributory causes. A recent UN report commenting on this situation noted that many people are prompted to leave their own country by a mixture of fears, hopes and aspirations which can be very difficult, if not impossible, to unravel.

Human Right Violations

As must now be abundantly clear, violations are the principal root cause of forcible displacement and respect for fundamental human rights is a key factor in the search for a durable solution to any situation of displacement. Violent internal conflicts in countries such as Colombia, Sierra Leone and Kosovo, in which civilians were and continue to be targeted and forced displacement is a deliberate tactic of warfare, lead to an ever-growing number of internally displaced persons.

Professor C. Mwabila Malela of the University of Kinshasa in the Democratic Republic of Congo has noted that "Africa is sinking because of bad political and economic choices made over the years"[7]. Although a handful of African leaders seem open to democracy, for example in Nigeria, Benin, South Africa and Senegal, others have personalised power, undermining national institutions of governance as they do so. According to Alison Des Forge, Human Rights Watch Consultant on Rwanda[8], "we have got used to a repressive system over the years. There are those who wish to hold on to power whatever it takes." Power has become synonymous with enriching oneself, and most wars are a scramble for the wealth Africa has to offer. Perhaps one of the reasons behind the emergence of critical situations is that the international community has focused too much on individual leaders as the

---

[7] In April 2000, a symposium on Africa was held at the Deusto University in Spain. The symposium, *Africa on the Threshold of the 21st Century*, was organised by the Institute of Human Rights, of the University of Deusto, JRS and Alboan, an international development agency based in Spain. For a summary of the presentations see JRS website: www.jesref.org under Africa Refugee Day.
[8] Ibid.

saviours of their respective countries rather than on the members of the whole civic society".[9]

Many of today's conflicts are characterised by mass human rights violations committed with impunity. Repugnant practices recur, like the recruitment of child soldiers and the use of anti-personnel landmines. Since ideological conflicts have dissipated with the fall of the Berlin wall, instigators of war have increasingly turned to the exploitation of ethnic identity to fuel their battles.

Setting the afflictions of Africa in a global context, we discover an impotence among international structures to address these conflicts. In terms of action for justice, the international community is weak. However, it is possible to set limits to the way conflict is conducted, to make it clear that mass killings as a way of keeping power are simply unacceptable. The International Criminal Tribunal on the Genocide in Rwanda offers a chance to hold those entrepreneurs of evil to account. Although its performance has been termed "less than spectacular", it at least offers the possibility of applying international legal standards. At a global level, while a statute for the establishment of an international criminal court was opened for signature in 1999, and 112 countries have become signatories, the court can only come into force when the statute has been ratified by 60 countries. Up until September 2000 19 countries had ratified the Rome Statute. One of the obstacles likely to delay the establishment of the court is current opposition by the United States.

In setting standards of accountability, one lesson the world should learn from Africa is that keeping silent in the face of widespread atrocities is the "greatest assistance one can give to evil doers". This is the conviction those who witnessed the

---

[9] On this particular point see also Trócaire Development Review 1998, Proceedings of Trócaire 25th Anniversary Conference on the theme *"People, Power and Participation – the Role of Human Rights Movements in Democratisation"*.

1994 Rwanda genocide came away with, notes Des Forges, adding that concrete and immediate steps can be taken by letting the world know what is happening. "People who are trying to change things from within must have support. The courage to denounce evil is hard to find and if one feels alone, it can be impossible."

Public denunciation is one means of intervention. Then there is the quiet, painstaking work of research undertaken by human rights investigators, taking information discreetly to a number of authorities. Another way of bearing witness to the suffering of victims of war is simply by being present alongside them. However, relief operations are rarely impartial. Philip Reyntjens of the University of Antwerp and Brussels[10] has noted that "Every humanitarian action has an impact in the context it is in, it is never neutral. This means that we have to be conscious of what we do and constantly informed of the context we work in, having always in mind the principle of 'preventing prejudice'. For JRS as an organisation based on faith and as an international body, a key task is to avoid being manipulated and to ensure that it, as an international agency, has a perspective which cuts across local divisions."

Another means of tackling situations of human rights violations is to use cultural strengths to build a peaceful society. Professor Mwabila notes that "It is through their culture that African countries can come to terms with themselves". Central characteristics of African cultures include fortitude and close family and community ties, along with a "total sharing" within a clan-based structure where no one exists alone. "In the absence of government, there are communities trying to manage their own affairs. In Mogadishu, Somalia, for example, the majority of schools are private enterprises," notes Dr Mudiappasamy Devadoss SJ of UNESCO. Civil society has also been heralded as a sign of hope as it gains ground in

---

[10] *Africa on the Threshold of the 21st Century*, Symposium, April 2000.

Africa, increasingly clamouring for accountability, democracy and peace. Des Forges sums this up by noting that "The hopeful signs are there, though they are not to be found in the circles of power, but among the people we work with".

Poverty is a form of Violence

While the incidence of persecution, armed conflict and human rights violations are obvious factors underlying forced displacement, they are not the only factors. What turns local conflicts into humanitarian disasters is poverty. People who live at the margins cannot survive long without a field to cultivate or a market in which to sell their produce. They have to move to keep alive.

Over the past three decades, the income differential between the richest and poorest fifth of the world's population has more than doubled, from 30:1 to 74:1[11]. In less developed regions of the world, no fewer than 89 countries now have lower *per capita* incomes than they had ten years ago. One fifth of the world's six billion people now live below the World Bank's official poverty line of a dollar a day.

The remedy offered by the International Monetary Fund and the World Bank to the poorest economies has included tough economic reform prescriptions under structural adjustment programmes. But these adjustment policies demanded by the world's most affluent states, whose views dominate decision-taking at the Fund and Bank, carry a high human and social price: unemployment, declining real wages, reduced public services and growing income differentials. The same countries with low and declining standards of living are particularly prone to complex emergencies, refugee outflows and other forms of forced displacement. Former President of Tanzania the late Julius Nyerere, making the link between poverty and

---

[11] UN Development Programme (UNDP), *Human Development Report 1999,* New York, Oxford University Press.

conflict in developing nations, noted that "poverty is like a gunpowder keg waiting to ignite".[12] And there is little room for optimism as the gross inequality of distribution of economic resources shows no sign of abating.

Conflicts

The immediate cause of forced displacement today remains the insecurity that arises out of conflict. Of the refugee situations where JRS works, only the Bhutanese refugees, of whom there are almost 100,000 in Nepal, did not result from direct conflict. According to the Stockholm International Peace Research Institute (SIPRI), the number of violent and destructive conflicts in Africa and around the globe is at its highest level since 1945. Refugee numbers have quadrupled since then, reaching a peak over the period 1993-95. Numbers would have climbed still higher, were it not for large-scale forced returns. Some 1.75 million Rwandan refugees were shunted back home to an unresolved situation.

SIPRI listed 27 major armed conflicts in 1998, only two - between India and Pakistan and between Eritrea and Ethiopia - were interstate. All the others were internal conflicts. Communal conflicts result from the breakdown of states, rising fundamentalism, the battle for scarce resources and from real or perceived inequalities. Where tribalism, ethno-nationalism or religious differences are evident, conflict is often fomented by ambitious leaders who appeal to ethnic or religious identity. Where power is contested, economic problems can provide opportunity for scapegoating. These phenomena are not new but appear to be on the increase rather than declining.

Yet these conflicts are also fuelled by western donor nations. World military expenditure in 1998 was about $700 billion and world arms production is highly concentrated among a

---

[12] Julius Nyrere addressing Concern Worldwide/Oxfam in Ireland conference, *Towards a European Common Foreign and Security Policy*, Dublin, November 1996.

few industrial countries. The major conventional arms suppliers for the period 1995 to 1999 were the USA, Russia, France, the UK and Germany. Indeed 80% of conventional arms exports come from those countries which constitute the five permanent members of the UN Security Council, the same countries charged with taking a lead role in promoting world peace[13].

A flourishing trade in both heavy weaponry and light arms is one of the principal threats to the national and regional security of Africa. The weapons arrive in exchange for diamonds, gold, timber and oil. Thus the international community is sucked into Africa's conflicts by its readiness to cash in on the continent 's natural resources.

Corruption, lack of efficient administration and poor infrastructure make governance both difficult and costly. The combination of weak states and rich natural resources has resulted in a dangerous environment which fuels conflicts. Western companies are also increasingly fuelling these conflicts without weighing the potentially disastrous consequences of their involvement. There are countless examples. Canadian Talisman or China Petrol are developing Southern Sudan's rich oil resources, seemingly forgetting over four million people displaced as a result of Sudan's civil war. The Dutch company De Beers has been accused of buying Angolan diamonds from rebel UNITA forces.

The weakening of the nation state

The collapse of national security and the weakening of the nation state are recurrent features in countries that experience conflict. Armed conflicts are characterised by fragmented political authority. Forced population displacements, inevitable during and after conflicts, in turn threaten regional, national and personal security. Despite the end of the Cold War and

---

[13] Stockholm International Peace Research Institute arms transfers database.

the so-called triumph of democracy, life has become increasingly difficult and dangerous for many populations since the super powers withdrew from their former 'stabilising' roles. A number of nation states have effectively collapsed, including Somalia, the former Yugoslavia, Liberia, Sierra Leone and of course, the former Soviet Union. Now Indonesia may be on the brink of a similar fate. Even the creation of new states - 27 in the last 10 years - is a sign of volatility. In many countries citizens have lost confidence in their government's ability or will to protect them. In Rwanda, Burundi and Liberia, the apparatus of government is controlled by minority factions that fail to treat everyone equally. Moreover, in fragile states when the economy declines or global forces shift the balance of power within a country, governments are tempted to react with force to control their people[14].

---

[14] See *Trócaire Development Review* 1999, section on Perspectives on Africa – The State and Civil Society.

4 Exile – Different Experiences and Different Challenges

Box 2

JRS volunteer: *Hello, how are you?*

Woman: *Fine thanks, although a little tired.*

Volunteer: *Would you like some water?*

Woman: *Thanks, only one bottle is enough.*

Volunteer: *If you want, take more than one.*

Woman: *No, thanks, we have another bottle of water and maybe you will need to give water to other families that do not have. Thanks again and thanks for coming, for waiting for us and for sharing bread and water.*

Volunteer: *Please, it is our obligation as human beings. Sorry for doing so little.*

(Dialogue between a refugee woman and a JRS worker in Albania, May 1999, on a train which carried refugees during the evacuation from Mieda to Fierz, southern Albania. The woman was travelling with four children and her old parents. The volunteer added: "She saw me and smiled, and then, taking my hands, cried softly. I cried too").

Who is a 'refugee? Broadening our understanding

The new forcibly displaced are often victims of the same conflicts and other forces which create refugees. But not all will fit the definition used by UNHCR. In the broader understanding developed by Catholic social teaching refugees are not only those in camps, but also include the internally displaced, the asylum seekers and homeless foreigners in urban settings, those imprisoned in immigration detention centres, and stateless persons.

The 1992 Vatican document *"Refugees: A Challenge to Solidarity"* developed this point as follows:

> *"Human conflicts and other life-threatening situations have given birth to different types of refugees. Among these are persons persecuted because of race, religion, membership of a particular social or political group. Only refugees in these categories are explicitly recognised by two important documents of the United Nations (1951 Convention and its Protocol). These juridical instruments do not protect many others whose human rights are equally disregarded."*

The document notes that

> *"in the categories of the International Convention are not included the victims of armed conflicts, erroneous economic policy or natural disasters. For humanitarian reasons, there is today a growing tendency to recognise such people as de facto refugees, given the involuntary nature of their migration. In the case of the so-called economic migrants, justice and equity demand that appropriate distinctions be made. Those who flee economic conditions that threaten their lives and physical safety must be treated differently from those who emigrate simply to improve their position."*

The document also points out that

> *" A great number of people are forcibly uprooted from their homes without crossing national frontiers. In fact during revolutions and counter-revolutions, the civilian population is often caught in the crossfire of guerrilla and government forces fighting each other for ideological reasons or for the ownership of land and national resources. For humanitarian reasons these displaced people should be considered as refugees in the same way as those formally recognised by the*

*1951 Convention because they are victims of the same
type of violence."*

Refugees living in camps

Many of the world's refugees live in specially created camps or
settlements. Providing care for and service to refugees in these
conditions requires intricate planning and well coordinated
efforts among UN agencies, NGOs, and any State authorities
that may be involved.

Those who suffer long-term displacement require food,
shelter, water, education, teacher training, social services,
women's development activities and health clinics. Refugee
camps range from small settlements of 50 persons – there are
over 100 small settlements for the Sri Lankan refugees in India
- up to camps of 150,000 or more, as those for Burundian
refugees living in Tanzania. Some refugees have no choice
but to exist in prisons patrolled by security forces, as did the
Vietnamese and Cambodians in Thailand and Malaysia.
Others are hosted within villages in neighbouring countries, as
many Liberians were accepted in Côte d'Ivoire and Guinea, or
Colombians in Venezuela

There are at least four sets of leadership/entities that need
to collaborate: the international community, usually
represented by UNHCR; the host country, sometimes
represented by its security forces; the service providers, which
are usually NGOs and the refugees themselves. Usually
formal agreements involve only the first three, and the refugee
population is left out. Sometimes refugee committees are
formed and even chosen in either democratic or traditional
ways. Sometimes there are resistance or militia leaders hidden
in the background who direct actions and dictate positions
taken by the refugees, as did the Rwandans in Kivu.

From the refugees' perspective, living in camp conditions is
fraught with unforeseen problems. Privacy is lost; so too may
be the refugees' sense of control over their lives. Divorced

from the routines and responsibilities of daily, independent living, refugees may find it difficult to maintain their self-respect, self-reliance and a belief in their own futures.

Internally displaced persons (IDPs)

A person becomes a refugee only when he/she crosses an international border. In contrast, an internally displaced person remains inside the boundaries of his/her own country. Thus, the difference between refugees and internally displaced persons is technical and legal, and has little to do with the reasons for flight. Both categories of persons are often affected by the same causes of displacement. They often have identical protection and material needs that deserve the equal attention of the international community.

The legal framework for the protection of IDPs includes human rights and humanitarian law as well as national legislation. In April 1998, the Commission on Human Rights adopted the Guiding Principles on Internal Displacement, which provide guidance to States and non State actors. Currently, Francis Deng is the UN's Special Representative for IDPs.

The Guiding Principles on Internal Displacement define IDPs as:

> *"persons or groups of persons who have been forced or obliged to flee or to leave their homes or places of habitual residence, in particular as a result of or in order to avoid the effects of armed conflict, situations of generalised violence, violations of human rights or natural or human-made disasters, and who have not crossed an internationally recognised State border."*

The Colombian Catholic Bishops recognise this phenomenon in their pastoral letter, "Displaced by Violence in Colombia":

> *"Internal displacement is a phenomenon in which persons and families who are not directly implicated in*

> *the fight suffer its grave consequences by finding*
> *themselves obligated to move from their places of*
> *origin to protect their lives ... If there is any group in*
> *Colombia whose human rights have largely been*
> *trampled, it is the displaced."*

The main problem facing humanitarian organisations in every conflict situation is how to reach internally displaced people. Fighting often makes it impossible to access an area, sometimes the terrain or meteorological conditions do not allow the passage of relief goods, and in other cases the whereabouts of victims are unknown. Frequently, difficulties in gaining access to those requiring assistance are not, however, a matter of unfortunate circumstances but are man-made and intentional. Looting of relief supplies, attacks on convoys, or refusal to authorise access can make it difficult for aid to reach its intended beneficiaries. The consequences can be disastrous, as events in Somalia, Bosnia and southern Sudan have shown.

The withholding of food and other vital goods is not a new phenomenon. As Christa Rottensteiner of the International Committee of the Red Cross (ICRC) explains:

> *"throughout history, starvation has been used as a*
> *method of warfare. The foremost goal of sieges and*
> *blockades was not to inflict suffering on the civilian*
> *population, which was seen as an inevitable "by-*
> *product", but to bring about the surrender of the enemy*
> *army. In today's wars, however, humanitarian*
> *assistance is increasingly denied as part of a deliberate*
> *policy to target civilians, in particular during internal*
> *armed conflicts. The often-discussed change in the*
> *nature of warfare might be one reason for this*
> *development. The other reason might be the change in*
> *the nature of humanitarian operations. In the 1990s,*
> *there has been an increasing tendency to use them as*

*a substitute for effective political or military action.
Over this period the number of relief operations has
risen steadily. This has led to a situation where
humanitarian assistance is often used as a bargaining
chip in political dealings and is therefore regularly
impeded. Because the international media is giving
more attention to the matter, the withholding of aid has
also become more obvious than before."*

Imprisoned immigrants

Many individuals fleeing across borders end up in immigration
detention centres, in need of legal counsel and pastoral care.
Their detention is at once a symptom of the breakdown in the
international system protecting refugees, and an indication of
many countries' failure to 'manage' migration. Detention is
used because constructive responses to the real (or imagined)
problem of the presence of foreigners are too elusive. For
detainees, stress exacerbates any pre-existing social,
psychological, spiritual and medical problems.

Mona Lazco, a JRS worker in Bangkok, writes about her
experience of saying goodbye to a group of Vietnamese boat
people released from the Special Detention Centre in
Bangkok:

*"On April 4 1997, after the closure of the last refugee
camps set up for the Vietnamese boat-people, those
who remained were transferred to the Special Detention
Centre (SDC) in Bangkok. The refugees lived at SDC
confined to their cells and no education was available
to the ten children in the group. Their departure was
very emotional. A 15 year old girl, Ms Haong, who had
never actually been to Vietnam before but was
nonetheless repatriated there today, said the following:
'I don't know what will happen to us when we return to
Vietnam. I am 15 years old but I have never been
there. What I hope for is that I can finally go to a real*

school and for the first time in my life I can also go to a church'."

This girl had spent all her life in refugee camps in Thailand and three years in the SDC.

Return, reintegration and imposed return

Another activity in which NGOs are acquiring considerable experience, is in accompanying refugees returning home - both in the preparation phase and during their return and reintegration. On return they are no longer refugees, but they are still displaced and still in need of protection. Post conflict returns, and the rehabilitation and reconstruction processes which accompany the transition from war to peace, require time, expertise, political will, solid financial support and considerable human resourcefulness. Since many of these returns are now precipitous and hastened by governments before the conditions at home are ripe, there is a role of accompaniment of populations who have returned home. Large repatriations in recent years include those to Namibia, Ethiopia, El Salvador, Guatemala, Cambodia, Mozambique, Rwanda, Liberia and Kosovo. Currently important are the returns of East Timorese, Sierra Leoneans, Rwandans and Bosnians. The return of Angolans has been halted by the resumption of conflict, and the return of the Bhutanese awaits negotiation. After any conflict, the processes required for successful reintegration and rehabilitation are long and arduous. Legal and education systems need to be rebuilt and housing and employment created. After war, orphans and widows abound. The deepest work of all, reconciliation and peace-building, takes decades, and starts only when the grief begins to ease. However, resources are often most readily available at the height of emergencies but become scarce when investment in long-term development is needed.

In the case of imposed return or *refoulement*, there are roles for independent and informed observers. Even when the return is not actually forced, it is important that standards be observed. In recent years UNHCR appears to have compromised its time honoured standards (that the return be voluntary, dignified and under safe conditions), and thus NGOs have felt compelled to speak out. This has occurred in the case of the Rohingyas returned from Bangladesh to Burma, the Rwandans returned from Tanzania, Aechenese returned to Indonesia from Malaysia, and some cases of Bosnians returned home from Germany.

Stateless persons

A rather new phenomenon, at least in its current proportions, and one which deserves a more coherent response, is that of stateless persons. There is a clear link between disputed nationality and forced displacement. Stateless persons suffer the double injury of being denied the right to return to their country of origin and being denied a nationality. Many of the Bhutanese refugees currently living in Nepal are, or risk being, in this category. There was a large caseload of Sino-Vietnamese in the Indo-Chinese camps, particularly in Hong Kong, who were certainly stateless. And in the former Soviet Union a large number of people have been left without a state to ensure that their basic human rights are upheld.

Although not all stateless persons who cross international borders are refugees, the 1951 Convention includes stateless persons in its definition of refugee. A stateless person is someone who *"not having a nationality and being outside the country of his or her former habitual residence as a result of such events, is unable or, owing to such fear, unwilling to return to it"*. UNHCR is the international body commissioned to implement the provisions of the Convention on Stateless Persons. The two primary international conventions on Statelessness are the 1954 Convention relating to the Status of Stateless Persons and the 1961 Convention on the Reduction of Statelessness, both developed under the auspices of the UN.

CHAPTER 5

Voices of women in exile – a gender perspective

"Eventually, I decided to leave Burundi. I was alone with my two children. We were crowded, together with many others, at the border between Burundi and Congo, waiting for a chance to escape the war. The only way to travel across the border was by bicycle-taxi.I carried one child on my back, and strapped the other against my chest, so we could all fit on one bicycle. With one hand, I balanced the bag containing all our belongings on my head, and with the other hand, I clung to the bicycle frame. By the time we reached the border, I had to lie down on the ground to recover, barely able to open my eyes. When we reached customs, we were searched for any items of value we may have, and were even undressed to make sure we had nothing hidden."

(Claire is a Burundian refugee who has since settled in Belgium)

The gender gaps in refugee policy

The large majority of refugees are women and children (about 80%). This is because the men are often fighting, or have been wounded or killed. At the same time responsibility for political decisions leading to war rests predominately with men. Although women do not die in as great numbers as men as a result of conflicts, war situations put women at risk from the "living deaths" of assault, rape, or loss of children.

Gender roles can shift dramatically in times of armed conflict. These shifts often challenge patriarchal power structures and destabilise interpersonal relationships between women and men and across generations. Dramatic demographic shifts also occur in wartime which impact on gender relations. The number of widows and female-headed households increases; and in the aftermath there is often a rise in polygamous marriages and in the birth rate. The economic changes brought about by war are equally dramatic. These include growing landlessness especially among women and the expansion of the informal sector as the number of jobs in the formal sector shrinks. These changes are the experience of Gabriela Cohen, an Angolan woman, who described the particular vulnerability of women in her country's conflict as follows: *"In 1994 when Bie was under siege by UNITA for 16 months, the only source of fuel and food was outside the city, across the front line. The civilian population organised small groups, often of girls, as they are normally responsible for collecting fuel, to run across the lines at night. Sometimes men used girls and women as shields, sending them in front to explode landmines."*

Females share the problems experienced by all refugees. But refugee women and girls also have special needs. They need protection against sexual and physical abuse and exploitation, and protection against discrimination in the delivery of goods and services, as the following account by a female refugee from Grozny highlights:

"In April 1996 I gave birth to a boy. When Grozny was shelled for the second time, our home was destroyed. For two long weeks, I hid myself in a cellar with my baby. Once water and food were exhausted, with my hope only in God, I got out of the city with the child, while the bomber planes were flying over our heads. It was just a miracle we were able to reach the town where my mother was living in the Dagestan Republic. When the war 'ended', my husband took us back to Chechnya, but as far as we were concerned, the war was still going on. One day, my husband did not come back from his work, and one month later he was

declared "disappeared". Again I brought my son to my mother, and I returned to Chechnya to look for my husband. One night four armed men broke into my house . They told me they had already killed my husband and that it was now my boy's turn. When they did not find him, they beat me and promised to come back. As I was pregnant, I was afraid that my new child, together with his older brother, would have to suffer for their father, so I decided to leave the country and search for a safe place for my sons, although I was unable to confirm my husband's death.

My second son was born in Spain. It is in this country that I hope to bring up my children, far from war and hatred. But I do not lose hope that we all might be reunited with their father one day."

Too often refugee women face dangers stemming from poor camp design,[15] for example, communal housing that provides no privacy for women; the location of basic services, such as latrines, at unsafe distances from the areas where refugee women are housed and poor lighting. In many refugee situations, strangers are thrown together while no efforts are made to restore traditional communities; unaccompanied women and female-headed households may be mixed in with those consisting of single men, and traditional mechanisms for ensuring order within the community may be broken down. Women may not have equal access to food and other distributed items in camps; they may have to walk great distances alone to obtain water and firewood; they may not have equal access to health care, education and skills training and income-generating activities.

Refugee women living outside camps, whether in urban environments or in village situations, also need protection

---

[15] Emiliana Tapia, *Refugee Women: A Kenya Case Study,* Trócaire Development Review 1999.

against human rights abuses. They might encounter problems related to lack of proper refugee documentation; difficulties in accessing education or training and income-generating activities; obstacles in gaining ownership of a leasehold on property; lack of access to social services; lack of information about the medical consequences of harmful traditional practices, such as female genital mutilation.

In Western societies, refugee women's voices are often ignored. Cultural ignorance can lead to a lack of respect for basic rights, as is illustrated by the case of Maryam:

> "The rape caused Maryam great pain and physical damage, as well as immense distress. Eventually the police let her go, but they told her that she would have to leave Somalia or she and her sons would be killed. And so Maryam came to Europe, and applied for asylum. She found the asylum interviews very distressing. At all stages of the procedure the interpreters, and nearly always the decision-makers, were men, which created an immense barrier for her to talk about her experiences in prison. She could only bring herself to speak in euphemisms –she had been "mistreated", "dishonoured". The asylum authorities refused to believe. She had to be lying, and her claim was "not credible."

Her request for asylum was rejected. Her appeal was refused too. She is now a "sans papier" and waiting to see if she will be allowed to stay for humanitarian reasons. She just found out she is HIV positive."

What hope lies ahead? Stories of Dignity

Education offers a real hope to break the ignorance and prejudice which results in violence against women. It can empower women and, by implication, empower men into a better understanding of human relations.

Women in situations of war and displacement are particularly vulnerable. To threaten a vulnerable person is to threaten the heart of our faith, even the heart of God. The scriptural exhortation to care for the widow and the orphan, the vulnerable with no one else to care for them, speaks loud and clear to our faith.

However, it would be a mistake to see women merely as victims. Some aspects of their experience are empowering and can be used as a resource for healing and transformation. The story of a woman from El Savador, Ana Amalia Guzman, bears eloquent testimony to the formidable strength of women in adversity. Amalia was detained in a US detention centre for 16 months for being an immigrant, separated from her husband, who was also detained, as well as being parted from her children. Amalia wrote of her imprisonment:

> "I had an encounter with Jesus personified; Romans made fun of Him, they took His clothes, they rejected Him. He was a prisoner and He suffered... I saw His passion when detainees were crying after being searched naked; I saw Him when detainees were fighting for their rights and justice, when they were suffering and in pain and nobody cared about it...My heart was broken and my hands were tied. I could do nothing to help them, I was just another detainee. In this situation, you just feel like dying. You don't know anything about your case, your future, how your family is doing. You are just waiting for the door to open to your freedom. When? Nobody knows. I experienced suffering and happiness, defeat and victory, but above all, I had the chance to share my feelings with other women. To me, that situation became a blessing, because I got the strength to fight and be able to survive, not giving up, no matter the circumstances; I had the privilege to help others in the worst moments of their life."

Such faith in the face of suffering, where Amalia used her pain to reach out to others, is a testimony we could all learn from and shows us that what we, who are not refugees, can bring is minimal in comparison to what we can receive. Refugees can be our teachers. The words of Anne Noeum Yak Tan show us the path to the healing of misery and brokenness brought about by war and a corrupt world:

> "My life is not easy now, but I do not despair. I hope in God. I believe God is my Father and will not abandon me. One day I shall join my husband and my children and we shall all be together again. Ten of my children are dead, and my husband has been killed, but I do not hold it against anyone. I have no spite against anyone at all. Nor did my husband hate the Khmer Rouge. He did not want to avenge himself for the evil they had done. I am like him. If I meet the one who killed my husband, I will not hate him, for I have no hate in my heart: I have accepted to strip myself of everything. In any case, I am not the only one to suffer. A whole people, a whole country suffers as well. But one day, I am sure, Cambodia will once again know happiness."

These words introduce "Watcher – what of the night", subtitled "The Little Book of the Dead", an extraordinary document by any reckoning. Noeum Yok Tan is the widow of Pierre Chuom Somchay, a Cambodian Christian who wrote a prayer in French on the reverse side of the baptismal certificate of ten of his twelve children, as one by one they succumbed to hunger and disease during the Pol Pot regime over the period 1975 to 1979. Finally he in turn was killed. In November 1979, while fighting was still going on, his wife Anne Noeum Yok Tan was able to carry the notes, walking for 20 days to the border, where she found safety in Khao-I-Dang refugee camp in Thailand. On the way she had the joy of finding her two surviving children.

In offering the booklet for others to read, Anne Noem Yok Tan's words echo with stunning simplicity the lives and memories of countless refugee families, none more so than the following short passage:

"When Somchay and I were together, he used to write. He wrote alone. He had learnt French when he was very young, since he was very gifted. He was a poet. I loved what he wrote so I have kept this little book with love. When I read it, my tears flow. He wrote it with the biros the children had brought with them when we left Phnom Penh. Poor children, they had taken what was most valuable to them, their school satchels, their exercise books, their biros, as if they were going to school."

PART II – TOWARDS A CHRISTIAN RESPONSE

CHAPTER

6 One family – journeying together

"Yes, war has changed our life, but not our spirit."

(Anna Huml, Bosnia)

In the place of origin: A ministry of peace and reconciliation

Refugees are individuals who have been forced to flee their homes, exiled and dispersed, to all four corners of our world. The Church worldwide consists of individuals who seek and build community. Homelessness is at the heart of the refugee experience, while hospitality is at the heart of the Church's mission. The two should be a perfect match.

The welcome given to a guest is the model for our encounters with refugees. A welcome is what refugees need; it is also the way we are invited to treat one another; and it is a recurring theme of the Bible. The visitors for whom Abraham, as a good bedouin, rushed to prepare restful shade and a refreshing meal at the oaks of Mamre were revealed as the messengers of God's promise. Whether the guest arrives at the expected time, or not — and the latter more common — we are invited to keep our lamps burning and watch faithfully and patiently (Mt 25:1–13; Lk 12:35). Normally our visitor arrives in the middle of the night and we must go 'importunately' to seek food from our neighbour (Mt 15:23; Lk 11:5). Always the quality of our welcome to the stranger — as a messenger from God — is the key criterion for our authentic faithfulness to God.

During his visit to a Palestinian refugee camp in March 2000, Pope John Paul II said:

"It is deeply significant that here, close to Bethlehem, I am meeting you, refugees and displaced persons, and representatives of the organisations and agencies involved in a true mission of mercy. (...) Dear refugees, do not think that your present condition makes you any less important in God's eyes! Never forget your dignity as his children... God's design was fulfilled in the midst of humility and poverty. Dear aid workers and volunteers, believe in the task that you are fulfilling. Genuine and practical solidarity with those in need is not a favour conceded, it is a demand of our shared humanity and a recognition of the dignity of every human being. The Church, through her social and charitable organisations, will continue to be at your side and to plead your cause before the world."

Many refugees are in shock. Many carry a deep sense of loss and grief. Many are humiliated, afraid, anxious, depressed or disoriented. Many feel wronged. Their tension is great. They are a people living on the edge, sometimes sceptical, often suspicious. Their family structure has in many cases been destroyed. Fathers may still be at war or may have been killed. Yet in all this, there is also a great will to keep families together and relationships intact.

On the journey – a ministry of accompaniment

The Church is practically everywhere. Not only can we welcome the refugee as she or he passes through our parish or diocese, but our international network can help protect them, follow them with care and help them to find a safe place of asylum. For this reason our role must complement that of various international organisations which do not always have this same access, either because of the specificity of their mandates or because of political obduracy. Wherever there is forced displacement, whether on a massive scale or one where even one family is placed at risk, the Church is often present. And the Church has a mission to accompany the outcast and to treat each person with respect.

To accompany means to be a companion. We as Christians seek for our own companions those with whom Christ prefers to be associated, the poor and the outcast. Etymologically speaking, 'companion' means 'one who shares bread'. In reality it expresses the commitment made in the Eucharist. The quality of companionship is well illustrated in Luke's account of two dejected disciples dragging their feet from Jerusalem to Emmaus, and finding a companion in the risen Jesus, though they could not at first recognise him. Christ walks with those who are searching and listens to them.

To accompany others is itself a practical and effective action. Frequently now this is the way refugee protection is provided. Accompanying refugees is a way to 'internationalise' a situation. The presence of an international team has been known to prevent attacks on refugees. When a free person chooses to accompany faithfully those who are not free — who have no choice but to be there — this is itself a sign, a way of eliciting hope.

Christianity has a striking message, that no person should be excluded, that all are neighbours deserving respect. Moreover, showing respect to the other person is the way to show respect to God. As St John Chrysostom said:

> *"It is only right that honour given to anyone should take the form most acceptable to the recipient not to the giver. Remember that he who said, 'This is my body', and made good his words, also said, 'You saw me hungry and gave me no food', and, 'in so far as you*

did it not to one of these, you did it not to me'. ... So give God the honour he asks for..."[16]

We must give our energy then to confront all sources of division and to respect and care for those who are excluded, of whatever religion, ethnic group or social class. We must work to prevent division, to care for those who journey, and to welcome those who arrive in our communities. Our practical commitment to refugees is the test of the authenticity of our faith. Not being a refugee, we do not dare to describe what it feels like to be uprooted in such a way. But we can describe what we see, hence the stories and testimonies of refugees which are transcribed throughout this text.

On arrival - a ministry of welcome

Agatha, a refugee from Rwanda who is now in Kenya, shows us how much there is in the Bible that relates to the experience of refugees. Reflecting on a text of the Deuteronomy she notes:

"The bible clearly tells us that God will never leave us or forsake us. God will remain with us through everything. Many refugees worry a lot about where we are going to sleep, what we are going to eat, where we will be tomorrow, but I would like to open up and tell you that the Lord will make you strong and help you; God will protect you (Isaiah 41). Scripture also tells us that unlike the birds in the air, we are especially privileged for God is there and ready to protect us. God is nearer to those who are discouraged and saves those who have lost hope. God preserves us so completely that not even one of our bones shall be broken. So my fellow refugees, place all your hope and put all your burdens on God, who fully

---

[16] From the homilies of St John Chrysostom (*Hom* 50, 3-4), Office of Readings for Saturday, 21st Week of the Year, *The Divine Office*.

understands each and every moment of our lives; keep on persevering, for one day we will be given rest. Truly God has heard our voice and sees our afflictions."

Migration, travelling in search of one's true home, the idea of life being a journey, is a familiar metaphor in the Bible and the Christian tradition. Another biblical theme, which is of great importance when thinking about strangers, exiles and refugees, is that of hospitality. In the societies which made up the worlds of the Old and New Testaments, as in many non-Western societies today, those who travelled or who moved away from home for any reason were dependent on the hospitality of the people among whom they found themselves. Today among Western cultures, hospitality has too often become an optional extra, and we are all impoverished for that.

Hospitality is a sign of friendship, an act of enrichment for both guest and host, an obligation to those who, like us, are made in the image of God and, therefore, are members of the same worldwide family. Judaism and Christianity do not have a monopoly in emphasising the virtue of hospitality: Muslims, Sikhs, Hindus, Buddhists and the followers of many other faiths all recognise the importance of hospitality.

Genesis chapter 18 provides us with a wonderful story, on the theme of hospitality. Abraham recognised the three travellers as messengers of God, and a son was born to Sarah and him just nine months later, as they had promised: a sign that hospitality and God's blessing go together. Generations later Abraham's descendants found themselves strangers and foreigners in Egypt. They had fled from famine, and were welcomed at first, but eventually fell into destitution and slavery. Their escape from slavery and their wanderings in the desert of Sinai, before they settled in Palestine, was an experience they have never forgotten. Modern Jews still celebrate Passover each year in commemoration of God's marvellous deliverance.

"Do not neglect to show hospitality to strangers", enjoins the New Testament writer to the Hebrews, in a reference to Abraham's story, *"for by doing that some have entertained angels without knowing it."* (Hebrews 13:2) The suffering of the Hebrew people which during their years in Egypt laid on them a moral obligation to be merciful to foreigners, strangers and exiles is described in the Book of Leviticus:

> *"When an alien resides with you in your land, you shall not oppress the alien. The alien who resides with you shall be to you as the citizen among you; you shall love the alien as yourself, for you were aliens in the land of Egypt."*
>
> (Leviticus 19:33-4).

St. Matthew tells the story of the Holy Family's flight into Egypt in order to emphasise Jesus' solidarity with his people: he had even shared symbolically in the exile that the Hebrew people had suffered long before. In his adult life, too, Jesus suffered homelessness. St. Luke records in his writings that, although the foxes had dens and birds their nests, Jesus had nowhere to lay his head.

St. Matthew also records a parable Jesus told about the way in which God will finally judge our conduct:

> *"When I was hungry, you gave me food; when thirsty you gave me drink; when I was a stranger, you took me into your home; when naked you clothed me; when I was ill, you came to my help; when in prison you visited me...anything you did for one of my brothers here, however humble, you did for me."*
>
> (Matthew 25:34-36, 40)

7 What we are called to do

*"The creation of small Christian communities has
helped to bring people from diverse areas together.
They have a chance to get to know one another, pray
the Bible together, and plan ways of helping each other
such as building shelters for the old and orphans. The
sharing of our lives in praying and in group counselling
helps to reduce emotional pain and bad thoughts, that
have come to us as a result of war which took so many
lives, including some of our relatives."*

(Kwizera Jena de Dew, a Burundi refugee in Tanzania)

The challenges displaced people provide to the Church, like
any challenges provoked by faith, come in many forms. First,
the experience of being a refugee is an offense to the dignity
of the human person. So we respond by insisting on that
dignity. The care of refugees offers a very special occasion for
a Christian to contact and give practical help to persons of
other faiths. More than half the refugees today, for example,
are Muslim. At the same time refugees show us how to be
true Christians and how to understand and live our faith. A
related task for the church is to arouse public opinion so that
more people will realise how human rights are violated with
impunity. A world where human rights are not respected will
continue to produce refugees of all kinds.

Finding hope and ending dependency

Considering the state of the world's refugees, we might ask
ourselves what hope there is for the world. Refugees can
teach us the human and central Christian truth, that hope
comes out from suffering, and even from despair. Philip
Gourevitch at the conclusion of his book, *We Wish to Inform
You That Tomorrow We Will Be Killed With Our Families*,
observes that "hope is a force more easy to name and declare

one's allegiance to than to enact". He concludes with the story of a man confessing on television to his participation in the killing of 17 schoolgirls and a 62 year old Belgian nun at a boarding school. The massacre was part of a Hutu Power liberation campaign. During the attack on the school,

> "the students, teenage girls who had been roused from their sleep, were ordered to separate themselves - Hutus from Tutsis. But the students had refused. The girls said they were simply Rwandans, so they were beaten and shot indiscriminately. Rwandans have no need - no room in their corpse crowded imaginations — for more martyrs. None of us does. But mightn't we all take some courage from the example of those brave Hutu girls who could have chosen to live, but chose instead to call themselves Rwandans?"

How can we accompany the refugees in a way that helps them to stand on their own two feet? *"Refugees are kneeling people"*, Guildo Dominici, a JRS worker, used to say when he was chaplain at the Vietnamese refugee camp of Galang Island in Indonesia.

The challenge for the pastoral worker is to establish a relationship of mutuality with those whom he or she serves. The pastoral worker must aim for a relationship that helps displaced people to stand free of dependency, especially when the displaced person has urgent needs. Certainly as a pastoral worker one can feel effective if one is 'loved' by the people. But let no one be deceived. One must not be loved only for the money or goods one brings.

Peter Hans Kolvenbach SJ sums this up as follows:

> "Because Christ chose to express his love for us by walking the road into exile and, later in his life, making the journey to Jerusalem to suffer torture and death (Luke 9:51-19:28), our service and presence in the midst of refugees, if rooted in fellowship with Christ,

can be a prophetic witness to God's love for us and make that love visible and tangible to those refugees who have not heard the Good News. This witness is the pastoral dimension of our work with refugees."

In order to survive a difficult situation, a refugee needs to see light at the end of the tunnel. He or she must have a contact with the outside, someone who cares, some sense that our confined situation is not their whole world, or some project to complete, an identification with a greater purpose. The risk in a refugee camp is that armed struggle will provide that sense of purpose. Refugee camps are classic recruiting grounds for rebel movements. Some movements deliberately maintain an environment of despair so that anger is sustained, to create a desperate will to fight and take risks.

For the one waiting in exile or in a refugee camp there is always time. For many it appears to be lost time, wasted time. The presence of pastoral workers can help a person to give time its meaning. Growth comes through taking the time needed for each part of our life, for mourning, for crying, for feeling anger, as well as for joy. Ecclesiastes 3.1 captures this where it is noted that

"There is a season for everything, a time for every occupation under heaven."

It is important to recognise that forced migrants are individuals from across the social and economic spectrum: professionals and skilled craftspeople as well as peasants and unskilled manual workers. By definition, they are people who escaped from intolerable situations in which others are trapped, and they had the strength and mental ability to survive what are frequently lengthy and dangerous journeys. There are therefore prima facie grounds for seeing them as more resourceful and enterprising than other people, rather than as pitiable cases.[17]

---

[17] Mark Leopold and Barbara Harell-Bond, "An Overview of the World Refugee Crisis", 1997.

In the poorer parts of the world, there are desperate skills shortages, and the potential role of refugees in overcoming them has been largely overlooked, as have the macroeconomic benefits of the presence of large potential refugee markets for basic goods (providing they are allowed to earn the money to pay for them). Much is made of the difficulties of integration into host societies, but ethnic diversity can be a culturally, as well as economically, enriching phenomenon (Hagen, 1988, Zetter, 1992).

Thus refugees need not be seen as either objects for our charity or threats to our livelihood, but as living people with something to contribute. They have a message that our world needs to hear. Pierre T de Chardin once said: "I think that the world will not be converted to the heavenly hope of Christianity if first Christianity does not convert itself to the hope of the world". We as members of a worldwide community are privileged to make that first step of conversion, through listening to the stories and hopes of the survivors of human conflict.

Christophe Renders SJ reflects on his friendship with the Rwandan refugees during his time in Bukavu, at the time when the refugees were being forced to go back to an insecure Rwanda:

> "Refugees have revealed to us the value of faithfulness. I was struck by their impression that they had been manipulated by everyone, particularly by the organisations who pretended to help them. In that state of spirit, it is not easy to say thank you. In the beginning it was very hard for me to accept their distance and mistrust. At the same time, there was a deep truth in their attitude. They have forced me to be "a useless servant, who only does his obligation… That is why when words or gestures of trust are transmitted, there is even more joy in receiving them. These signs showed that between them and us we were building a relationship beyond work. It was friendship."

Listening and Healing

Surely the only way to learn about the hope of a refugee is to listen to him or her. Our biggest temptation on seeing the distress of the refugees in camps or in a city like Johannesburg or Nairobi, is to begin projects, to give material things, to decide *en masse* what the refugees need. They often arrive in exile without shoes, with only one torn shirt, hungry, without a clear plan. But they did not undergo this experience in order to get a shirt or shoes. Their human experience calls for respect. They are traumatised by violence, lonely, rejected, exhausted in body certainly, but also exhausted by losing their place in a stable society — and sometimes feeling guilty about what they did in order to survive. The historical dimension of each person's experience of displacement of itself merits closer study, but is beyond the scope of this volume. Each displaced person wants to be understood, to be heard. Their frequent question is, 'Why is God doing this to me?' They have a right to ask this question. But it cannot be asked unless someone listens. This is our primary role, to listen to the questions, to the longing and to the fundamental human needs of refugees.

Often voluntary workers are the first and only people whom a refugee can trust after the trauma of flight. They left in fear and live in shock. We have a responsibility not only to listen but also to speak, and to facilitate communication. Refugees need to be informed and to learn the truth. Yet refugees are so often excluded from decisions concerning their lives.

One of the greatest sufferings of displaced people is losing contact with their loved ones. Great ingenuity is employed in passing messages and in finding out what is happening at home and among loved ones. We must do everything possible to open lines of communication and enable refugees to be well informed. Many times this service is reciprocated. They, in return, keep us much better informed.

Listening and learning is part of reconciliation. Reconciliation is not a developed art or ministry - but a pioneer field. Possibly the most effective reconciling actions are unselfconscious ones. Formation for peace can be integrated into our normal services. An agent of reconciliation must be close to the people, but may not take sides. With a Christian group, we can offer opportunities and conditions for a change of heart within a liturgical context. But even outside occasions of worship, depending on the culture, the community may be helped through theatre and dance, songs and choirs, counselling, and formation for teachers and other leaders. Reconciliation with one's own past involves remembering what happened, healing the memory and preparing for the future.

Pastoral Welcome – What makes for good practice?

Pope John XXIII, writing just one week before his death in 1963, noted that:

> "Today more than ever...we are called to serve man as such, and not merely Catholics; to defend the human person everywhere, and not merely the Catholic church...It is not that the Gospel has changed; it is that we have begun to understand it better...and to know that the moment has come to discern the signs of the times."

In providing pastoral support for refugees, certain classic principles apply. Basic among these is the refugees' fundamental right to freedom of worship, whether the refugees are Muslim, Buddhist or Christian. Conversely, no religious practice may be imposed on refugees by force, nor by 'blackmail' (subtle or not) such as offering assistance exclusively to those who attend religious services. A second principle is the right to worship in their own language and according to their own culture. Another principle involves respecting the duty of the local Christian community to welcome strangers who take refuge among them. These principles were also enunciated by the Commission for the Pastoral Care of Migrants in a 1992 publication:

"The responsibility of offering welcome, solidarity and assistance to refugees is incumbent, first of all, on the local Church. It is called to enflesh the Gospel demands by reaching out to them without distinction, when they are in need and where they are alone. This response will take different forms: personal contacts, defence of individuals and groups, denouncing injustices which are the root of the evil, lobbying for the passage of laws to guarantee effective protection, education against xenophobia, setting up volunteer groups and emergency funds, and the provision of spiritual aid."[18]

JRS in its programme of activities in the Cambodian camps in Thailand during the eighties, sought to help the monks re-establish their pagodas and schools, as well as to set up their own works of compassion associated with the wats (monasteries). This work was crucial at that time as the monkhood had been destroyed during the Pol Pot time, and its restoration was an essential means of assisting local communities to return to and to gain strength from their cultural and religious roots.

The biblical instructions on welcoming the stranger and exile are clear and consistently repeated. One of the most famous is the story of the Good Samaritan where the action of the Samaritan traveller on seeing the wounded man, is in stark contrast to the previous passers by. He is "moved with compassion at the sight" and risks being suspected of being the one who carried out the attack. He gives first aid and sees that the wounded man is properly cared for.

---

[18] *Refugees: A Challenge to Solidarity*, Pontifical Commission for Pastoral Care of Migrants, Rome, 1992.

When the lawyer sought a self-serving, definition of "neighbour," Jesus gave a stunning narrative in reply. His response effectively means: "You ask for an exclusive definition of 'neighbour'; my reply is: 'Be a neighbour to *anyone* who is in need." This response of Jesus is a challenge to go beyond our religious or ethnic group and to acknowledge and take seriously our membership in the human family.[19]

Other challenges

Supporting host communities

The vast majority of the world's refugees seek a safe haven in the poorest states. Countries in the developing world have long offered refuge to thousands of people fleeing en masse from persecution, civil conflict, violence, discrimination, and social and economic hardships. Sadly, this tradition of generosity has been changing in recent years, as countries close their doors to those seeking asylum. Many states appear to have forgotten that the right to "seek and enjoy in other countries asylum from persecution" is a fundamental and universal human right, and one which cannot be bargained away.

Countries in Africa have continued to offer asylum to the majority of the world's forcibly displaced. For example, Guinea proved a generous host to the largest single number of refugees in Africa in 1998 — a total of 430,000. In some parts of Guinea the refugee population actually outnumbered the host area's inhabitants. Some camps in Guinea had been cut off from assistance for several months, and malnutrition and mortality rates remained high. In 1998, according to UNHCR, only 1.5 per cent (360,850 people) of the total number of refugees classified as such by UNHCR (23 million) applied for asylum in European countries. The total number of people actually recognised as refugees in Europe during 1998 was 31,248.

---

[18] *Refugees, Those who travel under duress,* Mark Raper, JRS, 1998.

Even countries with a generous record of providing asylum have begun to shut their doors. Tanzania, for example, which has offered generous and extended asylum to several million refugees over the past thirty years, is tightening up its asylum policies. At the beginning of 1997 Tanzania forcibly returned 126 Burundian refugees following the outbreak of violence at a refugee camp. Of these refugees, 124 were killed by the Burundian army on arrival.

In light of this the challenge for governments, inter-governmental and non-governmental organisations, is to provide financial, material and technical assistance to all countries hosting large refugee populations. In the case of large-scale influxes, such assistance should be provided on a timely basis in order that lives are not lost and to ensure that host countries are not forced to close their borders to prevent further influxes of refugees.

Burden sharing should also extend to redressing the negative impact of refugees on host communities. All costs and damage which host countries would not have suffered but for refugees should appropriately be seen as a joint responsibility of the international community. In developed countries, refugees and asylum seekers are often housed in areas of social disadvantage and exclusion. Taking an integrated approach, which includes education, planning with and learning the issues facing host communities as well as refugees, is important in achieving successful integration.

Enhancing non-refoulement

The debate about the conditions under which refugees return home is one of the most controversial issues in refugee policy. The principle of voluntariness had been held up as the cornerstone of international refugee protection and the most important safeguard against the imposed return of refugees to countries where they could face persecution. In practice, however, as the examples of Burma and Rwanda illustrate, we are witness to incidents where refugees are forced to return to conditions of extreme insecurity where respect for their fundamental rights cannot be guaranteed.

Rejected asylum seekers are often returned to what are erroneously said to be safe countries of origin. An alarming practice in this respect is the use by certain western countries of so-called "white lists", wherein certain countries are deemed not to produce asylum seekers. This goes against international human rights law, as the right to seek asylum should be available to every human being irrespective of where they live or come from. Another disturbing practice is the return of asylum seekers to the so-called "safe third countries". There is a danger of chain deportations when people are sent to a "safe third country" without proper assurances that their asylum application will be correctly examined there.

A core challenge as states, and unfortunately UNHCR, adhere less and less frequently to the principle of voluntariness, is to re-examine urgently international standards in order to ensure that refugees are not forcibly returned to conditions where their basic rights and security are at risk, and to ensure that the fundamental principle of non-refoulement is always upheld. Return should take place only to rights-respecting environments, within a clear human rights framework and according to clearly defined international human rights standards.

Defending Human Rights

"A refugee situation is a difficult one. We are people with many problems. Our rights are not respected in our land of origin and often neither in the land of asylum. We are without a voice and when we try to speak, our voices are not heard. But we have our lives and that is our biggest hope. We shall one day return to our home land, where there will be peace for all and

*we shall live together, build our lives anew, and have a
chance to plan for our lives and our future."*

(Kwizera Jean de Dew, a Burundian refugee in Tanzania)

The link between respecting human rights and the protection
of refugees is self-evident. People are displaced as a result of
human rights violations. Their rights are frequently violated
during displacement. And seeking a solution to their
displacement entails ensuring a restoration of and respect for
their basic rights.

Obvious though it may seem, the link between human rights
and forced displacement has only begun to receive concerted
international attention in recent years. There is a growing
realisation among governments and international
humanitarian and human rights organisations alike that
human rights are central to any efforts to prevent, respond or
seek solutions to, problems of forced displacement. The role
of international human rights organisations, including
churches, in shaping this opinion and highlighting the
fundamental connection between human rights and forced
displacement remains vitally important.

Campaigns, research projects and public education must be
undertaken to defend the rights of refugees. From their field
experience, for example, many NGOs and church groups
have joined forces in opposition to the spread of small
weapons, notably anti-personnel landmines. They speak up for
stateless persons and defend the rights of children forced into
war. They highlight the decline of protection for refugees in
camps, such as in cases when camps are militarised or their
civilian nature is not properly controlled; or when women are
at risk; or when camps are located so that they are vulnerable
to cross border attacks. NGOs offer critical comment
regarding UNHCR and government policies and practice, for
example, regarding urban asylum seekers, detention of asylum
seekers, and procedures for determining refugee status.

If we listen to the refugees and discern what they say to us, their message can be better heard. We are not so much a 'voice for the voiceless', but assist those without voice to express themselves. They have a primary right to speak on their own behalf. Finding ways to facilitate their communication is a challenge to our creativity. Meanwhile, simply by being with them we give witness to their situation and we call attention to what is happening.

Lisbert D'Souza SJ, Provincial of the South Asia Jesuit Conference, has this to say:

> "Surely there is also power for good? ... The shocking violations of human rights of individuals and social groups and even of nations, take place because they are powerless. How can I use such minuscule power as I possess to defend the defenceless, and aid the powerless? Jesus' exercise of power in his miracles was not a show of strength; it was a sign of the Kingdom. But his greatest sign of the Kingdom was not in power but in powerlessness. Perhaps the powerless will be helped most not by my use of power, even in their favour, but in surrendering it to be powerless like them and with them. To believe this, to act on it is the biggest challenge I face as the millennium runs to it close."

Ending xenophobia

> "Perhaps, yes, it is xenophobia, but who has not the right of being xenophobic?"

This was written in a daily newspaper in Malta, in an article criticising the weaknesses of the 1951 Refugee Convention as being too liberal. The response to this article, published in the same newspaper stated:

> "Xenophobia is described as "fear or hatred of foreigners", a xenophobe "one who fears or hates

*foreigners". Hatred is not a right. If fear is based on
stereotypes and prejudices, then it is certainly not a
right. Sadly, fear of foreigners is all too often based on
stereotypes and prejudices, on assumptions which are
just that, assumptions, many built on half baked truths,
others built on myths, others blatant lies."*

As Human Rights Watch reports regularly reveal, among states
around the world from Tanzania to Thailand to Turkey, there is
a growing wave of anti-refugee sentiment and xenophobia.
No country wants refugees. They are viewed as a drain on
scarce economic resources, a strain on the environment, and
a threat to national and regional security. Refugees are
stigmatised because they are ethnically, racially or socially
different. Often refugees are from unpopular ethnic minority
groups (Hutu Rwandans in Tanzania; Iraqi Kurds in Turkey;,
Burmese ethnic minority groups in Thailand). In Western
Europe and North America, refugees from Africa, Asia, Latin
America, and the Middle East are frequently racially different
from the majority population; or they come from socially
stigmatised and excluded groups (Albanians in Italy; the Roma
in Hungary; the Kurds in Germany).

Race and refugee policy are inextricably linked. In some
instances refugees are forced to flee precisely because of their
race and ethnicity. Indeed, the refugee definition in the 1951
Convention includes persecution on the grounds of race.
Examples of refugees forced to flee because of racial
persecution include the Roma in central and Eastern Europe,
the black Mauritanians in Senegal and Mali, and Bhutanese
refugees in Nepal.

Even where race is not a causal factor in the flight of
refugees; it is certainly a determining factor in how refugees
are treated and in public perceptions and attitudes. Some of
the worst racist attacks in Germany, for example, have been
targeted at hostels for asylum seekers. In Kenya, in a clearly
xenophobic attack on foreigners, President Moi unilaterally

blamed refugees for the rise in crime in the country. In the UK, asylum seekers (especially those from West Africa) were repeatedly portrayed as "scroungers" and "cheats" in the popular tabloid press, and were consequently stripped of rights to welfare benefits. In Ireland refugees and asylum seekers have also met with screaming newspaper headlines and untrue stories. In Ireland, after campaigning by political, church, trade union and non-governmental groups, certain asylum seekers have been allowed to work. Not being allowed to work or engage in formal study in Ireland as elsewhere has severely limited the capacity of asylum seekers to integrate into their host communities and has created a perception that they are "scrounging", thus fuelling racism.

In Africa, the growth of xenophobia is happening at the time when virtually all countries have adopted democratic forms of government. As UNHCR has observed, "because of the democratisation process, governments increasingly accountable to the public opinion may be tempted to tighten their refugee policies in response to these negative perceptions ..." South Africa and Tanzania are two examples where public opinion has negatively influenced refugee policy. Hence the importance of civic education programmes and building a culture of respect for human rights.

After closing its borders with Burundi and Rwanda to prevent further influxes of refugees, the Government of Tanzania cited the interdiction by United States of the Haitian and Cuban refugees to justify its action. The then Minister for Foreign Affairs said that it was a double standard to expect weaker countries to live up to their humanitarian obligations, as major powers did not do so when their national rights and interests were at stake.

The link between xenophobia and racism is one that should be explored. Governments' refugee policies should be examined to ensure that they do not discriminate on racial grounds, and where necessary should be scrutinised under the relevant UN mechanisms pertaining to racial discrimination. The growth of xenophobia arises primarily out of the failure of the public to appreciate the situation of refugees. It is indeed a communications and education problem. Accordingly, the best way to tackle the problem of xenophobia is through public awareness campaigns and education at all levels of society, pointing out the positive contribution that refugees can make to host countries. Church groups must play an important role in this.

Addressing root causes

Violence and conflict are the principal causes of forced displacement, but external factors contribute to forcible population displacement too, particularly the inequitable international economic system which has damaged already fragile economic systems. Addressing the above problems requires a political and economic agenda aimed at eliminating ethnic strife and conflict; curtailing the arms trade; establishing a firm foundation for democratic institutions and governance; respect for human rights; the promotion of economic development and social progress.

Refugee flows are not a consequence of anonymous or abstract historical forces. They are a result of deliberate actions taken by states and individuals, which sometimes have population displacement as their very purpose. The only way to deal with this cause of forced migration is to hold those states and individuals accountable for their actions under the doctrine of state responsibility and the emerging principles of criminal responsibility under international law.

PART III CONCLUDING REFLECTIONS

Obviously the actions of any individual may seem insignificant compared to the problems of refugees described in this booklet. But all actions matter. And the actions of a community, especially as part of a worldwide community of solidarity, are never insignificant; they are more than the sum of the parts. To accompany an otherwise forgotten refugee is not time wasted. It is a privilege. Time spent listening to the story of a refugee like Anne Noeum Yok Tan cannot be time wasted. The lesson of the Rwandan girls is a lesson for more than just Rwanda. The world needs such grounds for hope and such a vision that will lead it out of its conflicts. Welcoming and serving the foreigner, especially the refugee, is the way in which we can be and are truly Christian.

Do we bring hope to refugees or do we find it in their midst? The richness of human spirit that we discover among refugees, including a vibrant hope, is always a surprise. Obviously there is sadness in the exile's song, as Psalm 136 recalls: *"By the rivers of Babylon there we sat and wept, remembering Sion"*. The longing is tangible, a longing to see the 'Holy City'. While there may be no rational grounds for believing that what a refugee longs for will actually come about, we may also find hope in the other's hope. For hope is not optimism. Optimism expects that things will get better. Hope is a virtue grounded in suffering. It is a grace that gives strength. Hope is a promise that takes root in the heart and is a guide to an unknown future. The challenge is to search for and find the seeds of hope, to allow these to grow, to fan the feeble spark into a flame, and to help change a refugee camp from something to survive in to a time and place for growth. Hope is what enables us to live fully in the present moment.

The experience of being a refugee is an offense to the dignity of the human person. So we respond by insisting on that dignity. We should offer

> "love and assistance to all refugees without distinction as to religion or race, respecting in each of them the inalienable dignity of the human person created in the image of God."[20]

Non-government organisations and the churches need to become stronger and more central in the international response to refugees and forcibly displaced people. Priority must be given to strengthening civil society, especially local human rights organisations and to supporting local communities with a concern for human dignity and wellbeing, including women's movements, village organisations and co-operative associations. But all of these local organisations need to be linked through reliable and trustworthy communications to international counterparts, both for their own safety and for their effectiveness.

The example of the Nobel Prize winning international landmines campaign is revealing. This campaign chose to by-pass the unwieldy and intensely partisan UN process of securing votes for a revised international Convention. Instead, it succeeded in weaving a network of new alliances between individuals, non-government movements and governments. Through this alliance, pressure was exerted even on non-state parties to conflicts, such as rebel and resistance movements. The same type of campaigns and alliances are needed now to combat many other harmful and inhumane phenomena that create and accompany forced displacement, such as the proliferation of small weapons, the recruitment of children into armies, the trade across frontiers in human beings. In order to fulfil the same mission of service to and protection of the forcibly displaced and the victims of humanitarian crises, non-government organisations need to extend their services and advocacy to encompass a wider range of activities.

---

[20] I Rifugiati, Una sfida alla solidarietà, Pontifical Council for the Pastoral Care of Migrants and Itinerant People, 1992, #1.

During his visit to a Palestinian refugee camp in March 2000, Pope John Paul II said:

"The degrading conditions in which refugees often have to live; the continuation over long periods of situations that are barely tolerable in emergencies or for a brief time of transit; the fact that displaced persons are obliged to remain for years in settlement camps: these are a measure of the urgent need for a just solution to the underlying causes of the problem. I plead with all who are sincerely working for justice and peace not to lose heart. I appeal to political leaders to implement agreements already arrived at, and to go forward towards the peace for which all reasonable men and women yearn, to the justice to which they have an inalienable right."

The words of Peter Hosking of JRS East Timor provide a message of hope to us all as global citizens and remind us that while global changes are needed to end the abuses which give rise to refugee movements, individual actions of solidarity can also help change the lives of refugees and those who accompany them in the meantime. He writes:

"There are many skills to be learnt, but perhaps at the end of the day it is a vocation of accompaniment or healing. It is a gift, and never something that belongs to us. It is not something we can presume upon because of our talent or skills. It is simply the trust to be with another knowing that each of us is created in love and that our destiny is to return to the fullness of love, but what happens in between is often a huge struggle. A bigger struggle for some than others. A struggle made harder because of the wanton cruelty of people. But my abiding feeling is a deep knowledge that love triumphs eventually".

Glossary of terms

Asylum: the granting, by a State, of protection in its territory to a person/persons from another State who is/are fleeing persecution or serious danger. A person who is granted asylum is a refugee. Asylum encompasses a variety of elements, including *non-refoulement,* permission to remain on the territory of the asylum country, and humane standards of treatment.

Asylum seekers: those individuals who formally request permission to live in another State because they (and often their families) have a "well founded fear of persecution" in their country of origin. This distinguishes them from migrants in general.

Cartagena Declaration on Refugees: a Declaration adopted by a colloquium of experts from the Americas in November 1984. The Declaration enlarges the refugee definition to include "…persons who have fled their country because their lives, safety or freedom have been threatened by generalised violence, foreign aggression, internal conflicts, massive violation of human rights or other circumstances which have seriously disturbed public order". While the Cartagena Declaration is not a treaty, its provisions are respected across Central America and have been incorporated in some national laws.

Cessation clauses: legal provisions that indicate when refugee status comes to an end. Cessation clauses are found in Article 1c of the 1951 Convention, and in Article 1 (4) of the 1969 OAU Convention.

Convention on the Reduction of Statelessness: a Convention that provides for the acquisition of nationality by those who would otherwise be stateless and who have an appropriate link with the State through birth in the territory or through descent from a national. The Convention also provides for the retention of nationality by those who would become stateless if they were to lose the State's nationality. The Convention was adopted in August 1961 and came into force in December 1975. UNHCR has been mandated with specific functions under Article 11 of the 1961 Convention on the Reduction of Statelessness.

Convention relating to the Status of Refugees: a Convention that establishes the most widely applicable framework for the protection of refugees. The Convention was adopted in July 1951 and entered into force in April 1954. Article 1 of the 1951 Convention limits its scope to "events occurring before 1 January 1951". This restriction is removed by the 1967 Protocol relating to the Status of Refugees. To date, there are 139 States who are parties to the 1951 and/or the 1967 Protocol.

Convention relating to the Status of Stateless Persons: a Convention that provides the definition of a stateless person and establishes a framework by which a stateless person who is lawfully resident in a State can have legal status. The Convention was adopted in September 1954 and came into force in June 1960.

Convention refugees: persons recognised as refugees by States under the criteria in Article 1 A of the 1951 Convention, and entitled to the enjoyment of a variety of rights under that Convention.

Country of first asylum: a country in which an asylum seeker has been granted international protection as an asylum seeker or a refugee.

Customary international law: laws that derive their authority from the constant and consistent practice of States, rather than from formal expression in a treaty or legal text.

Durable solutions: any means by which the situation of refugees can be satisfactorily and permanently resolved to enable them to live normal lives. UNHCR traditionally pursues the durable solutions of voluntary repatriation, local integration and resettlement.

Gender-related persecution: persecution that targets or disproportionately affects a particular gender. Under certain factual circumstances, gender-related persecution may come within the refugee definition.

Guiding Principles of Internal Displacement: a series of principles that articulates standards for protection, assistance and solutions for internally displaced persons. The Guiding Principles were presented to the Commission on Human Rights by the Representative of the Secretary General for Internally Displaced Persons in April 1998. They reflect and are consistent with human rights law, humanitarian law and refugee law, and provide guidance to States, other authorities, intergovernmental, and non-governmental organisations faced with issues of internal displacement.

Internal Displacement: involuntary movement of people inside their own country. This movement may be due to a variety of causes, including natural or human-made disasters, armed conflict, or situations of generalised violence.

Internally Displaced Persons: those persons forced or obliged to flee from their homes, "…in particular as a result of or in order to avoid the effects of armed conflicts, situations of generalised violence, violations of human rights or natural or human-made disasters, and who have not crossed an internationally recognised State border" (according to the *Guiding Principles of Internal Displacement*)

Local integration: a durable solution to the problem of refugees, which involves their permanent settlement in a country of first asylum.

Mandate refugees: persons who are recognised as refugees by UNHCR acting under the authority of its Statute and relevant UN General Assembly resolutions. Mandate status is especially significant in States that are not parties to the 1951 Convention or its 1967 Protocol.

Non-refoulement: a core principle of refugee law that prohibits States from returning refugees in any manner whatsoever to countries or territories in which their lives or freedom may be threatened. The principle of *non-refoulement* is a part of customary international law and is therefore binding on all States, whether or not they are parties to the 1951 Convention.

OAU (Organisation of African Unity) Convention Governing the Specific Aspects of Refugee Problems in Africa: the regional complement to the 1951 Convention whose refugee definition is broader than that provided in the 1951 Convention. Adopted in 1969, the OAU Convention provides that "the term 'refugee' applies to those fleeing from external aggression, occupation, foreign domination or events seriously disturbing public order in either part or whole of the country of origin".

Particular social group (membership of a ...): one of five possible grounds on which persecution may be established under the 1951 Convention. A particular social group would have distinct characteristics that set the group apart. Persons belonging to the group would share defining characteristics that may be innate or acquired (for example, interests, values, behaviour, or backgrounds). The defining characteristics would be such that relinquishing them would entail violating the basic human rights of the individuals concerned.

Persecution: generally refers to any severe violation of human rights. In the refugee context, "persecution" refers to any act by which fundamental rights are severely violated for reasons of race, religion, nationality, political opinion or membership of a particular social group.

Prima facie determination of refugee status (or group determination of refugee status): a practice by which all persons forming part of a large-scale influx are regarded as refugees on a *prima facie* basis. Group determination ensures that protection and assistance needs are met without prior individual status determination.

Refoulement: the removal of a person to a territory where she/he would be at risk of being persecuted, or of being moved to another territory where she/he would face persecution. *Refoulement* constitutes a violation of the principle of *non-refoulement*, and is therefore a breach of refugee law and of customary international law.

Refugee law: the body of customary international law and various international, regional and national instruments that establish standards for refugee protection. The cornerstone of refugee law is the 1951 Convention relating to the Status of Refugees.

Refugee status determination procedures: legal and administrative procedures undertaken by UNHCR and/or States to determine whether an individual should be recognised as a refugee in accordance with national and international law.

Repatriation/Reintegration: the process by which refugees resume a normal life in their country of origin. Ideally, reintegration should follow from the durable solution of voluntary repatriation.

Resettlement: the transfer of refugees from the country in which they have sought refuge to another State that has agreed to admit them. The refugees will usually be granted asylum or some other form of long-term resident rights and, in many cases, will have the opportunity to become naturalised citizens. For this reason, resettlement is a durable solution as well as a tool for the protection of refugees.

Resettlement country: a country that offers opportunities for the permanent resettlement of refugees. This would be a country other than the country of origin or the country in which refugee status was first recognised.

Safe areas/safety zones: areas, zones, or locations established to protect civilians during a time of conflict. The terms and conditions of establishing safety zones are governed by the law of armed conflict.

Safe third country: a country in which an asylum seeker could have found protection as a refugee, and in which she/he has been physically present prior to arriving in the country in which she/he is applying for asylum.

Stateless person: a person who is not considered a national by any State under the operation of its law.

Temporary protection: an arrangement or device developed by States to offer protection of a temporary nature to persons arriving en masse from situations of conflict or generalised violence, without prior individual status determination. Temporary protection was applied in some Western European States for the protection of persons fleeing the conflict in the former Yugoslavia in the early 1990s.

Unaccompanied minors: persons below the legal age of majority who are not in the company of parents, guardians or primary care-givers.

UNHCR mandate: the role and functions of UNHCR as set forth in the UNHCR Statute and as elaborated in resolutions of the United Nations General Assembly. UNHCR's mandate under its Statute is to pursue protection, assistance and solutions for refugees. UNHCR has an additional mandate concerning issues of statelessness, as it is given a designated role under Article 11 of the 1961 Convention on the Reduction of Statelessness. The Office has also been requested by the General Assembly to promote the 1954 and 1961 statelessness Conventions, and to help prevent statelessness by providing States with technical and advisory services on nationality legislation and practice.

Voluntary repatriation: return to the country of origin based on the refugees' free and informed decision. Voluntary repatriation may be organised, (i.e., when it takes place under the auspices of the concerned governments and UNHCR), or spontaneous (i.e., the refugees return by their own means with UNHCR and governments having little or no direct involvement in the process of return).

Women-at-risk: female refugees with special protection needs, including those who require resettlement in accordance with UNHCR Resettlement Handbook.

Bibliography

An overview of the World Refugee Crisis, Mark Leopold and
  Barbara Harell-Bond, 1997

Forced Displacement Today and The Pastoral Challenge to the
  Church, Mark Raper SJ, Facultà Teologica, Cagliari, March
  1998

Los refugiados de los Grandes Lagos, Jesuit Refugee Service-
  Grands Lacs, Política Exterior, July-August 2000

"Migrants and their Irregular Situation", John Paul II, July 1995

Protecting Refugees: A Field Guide for NGOs, produced jointly
  by UNHCR and its NGO partners

Pastoral Accompaniment among Refugees - The Jesuit Refugee
  Service experience, Mark Raper SJ, September 1998

Populations Displaced: An Overview of Refugees and Forcibly
  Displaced People Today. Notes for a talk at Bielefeld
  University, by Mark Raper, Working Paper n.311, Sociology
  of Development Research Centre, Universitat Bielefeld.

Refugees: A Challenge to Solidarity, Pontifical Council for the
  Pastoral Care of Migrants and Itinerant People, 1992

Refugees: Those who travel under duress, Mark Raper SJ, The
  Way, January 1999

Refugee status determination practices in the Philippines,
  Thailand and Cambodia, by Michael Alexander. Published in
  the International Journal of Refugee Law, Volume 11,
  Number 2, 1999

Report 1999, International Peace Research Institute (SIPRI)

UNHCR Working Paper No.5: "The end of asylum? The
  changing nature of refugee policies in Africa", Bonaventure
  Rutinwa, Refugee Studies Programme, Oxford, May 1999

Watcher, what of the night?, Mark Raper SJ, published in
  Priests & People, February 2000

World Report 2000, Human Rights Watch

Books for Further Reading
The State of the World's Refugees 1997-98, UNHCR, published by Oxford University Press.

Voluntary Repatriation: International Protection, a Handbook produced by the General Legal Advice Section of UNHCR

UNHCR Resettlement Handbook, produced by the UNHCR Division of International Protection

Working for Reconciliation, a Caritas Handbook, Caritas Internationalis

Refugees and Asylum Seekers, A Challenge to Solidarity, Irish Commission for Justice and Peace/Trócaire, 1997.

Gender related literature
Guidelines on the Protection of Refugee Women, published by UNHCR.

Sexual Violence against Refugees-Guidelines on Prevention and Response, produced by UNHCR.

Women asylum seekers-A Legal Handbook, published by Immigration Law Practitioners' Association and Refugee Action, 1997.

Refugee Women: A Kenya Case Study, Emiliana Tapia, Trócaire Development Review 1999.

Children
Refugee Children: Guidelines on Protection and Care, published by UNHCR

Training Modules prepared for the Action for the Rights of Children (ARC) project

Implementation Handbook for the Convention on the Rights of the Child, published by UNICEF

Report on the Impact of Armed Conflict on Children, by Graça Machel, published by UNICEF (and accessible via the UNICEF website)

Useful web sites

UNHCR:
http://www.unchr.ch/

United Nations High Commissioner for Human Rights:
http://www.unhchr.ch/

UNICEF:
www.unicef.org/

Caritas Internationalis:
http://www.caritas.org/

Oxfam:
http://www.oneworld.org/oxfam/

CAFOD:
http://www.cafod.org.uk/

Trócaire:
http://www.Trócaire.org/

Save the Children:
http://www.savethechildren.net/

Human Rights Watch:
http://www.hrw.org/

Amnesty International:
http://www.amnesty.org/

Global Witness:
http://www.oneworld.org/globalwitness/

Lawyers Committee for Human Rights:
http://www.lchr.org/home.htm

Refugees International:
http://www.refintl.org/

Global IDP Database:
http://tornado.jstechno.ch/nrc/nrcdefault.html

Jesuit Refugee Service:
http://www.jesref.org/